Nina,
Thanks for the support!
I hope you enjoy the book.
All the best,

Lessons from Legends

---

12 HALL OF FAME COACHES ON LEADERSHIP, LIFE, AND LEAVING A LEGACY

with Scott Bedgood

Front Cover Design: Kinsey Stewart
Edited by: Jon Finkel

Cover Photo Credits
Barry Alvarez – David Stluka/Wisconsin Athletic Communications
Mike Bellotti – Eric Evans/GoDucks.com
Marino Casem –Alcorn State Athletics
Fisher DeBerry – Air Force Athletics
Terry Donahue – Don Liebig/UCLA Athletics
Vince Dooley – Fred Bennett
Phil Fulmer – Donald Page/Tennessee Athletics
Frank Girardi – Lycoming Athletics
Tom Osborne – Nebraska Athletics
R.C. Slocum – Glen Johnson/Texas A&M Athletics
Steve Spurrier – Florida Athletics
Barry Switzer – Oklahoma Athletics

Lessons from Legends/ Scott Bedgood. —1st ed.
ISBN 978-0-692-94768-5

Contents

i

To my wife, Sami, my family, and Coach Courtney.

A coach is someone who tells you what you don't want to hear, who has you see what you don't want to see, so you can be who you have always known you could be.

—Tom Landry

Praise for the Coaches

BARRY ALVAREZ

"I learned a lot of great lessons from Coach Alvarez, but there are two that are by far the best to me. First, don't flinch. A lot of people in life, when they're faced with a moment of adversity, tend to flinch and redefine themselves by trying to overthink the situation. Your first and initial reaction is always the best. The second lesson was to enjoy every win. I don't care if it's over the No. 1 team in the nation or an FCS opponent, you need to enjoy every one of them fully." – **Bret Bielema, Arkansas Head Coach and former Wisconsin assistant under Alvarez**

TOM OSBORNE

"It was an incredible honor to play for and be coached by Tom Osborne. Coach taught us about teamwork and the value of 'unity of purpose.' Each person connected to the program was valued and played an important role in the overall success of Nebraska football. We also learned about the importance of being a great student and how to be an active participant in the community. We learned to respect the game, to honor those who came before us by our work ethic, and by our habits. In short, we participated in a lot more than wins and losses- we learned how to become leaders. I could not be more proud to say that Tom Osborne was my Coach." – **Trev Alberts, Nebraska-Omaha Athletics Director, Nebraska LB; Butkus Award, Lambert Trophy Winner; College Football Hall of Famer**

BARRY SWITZER

"Coach Switzer had a way of motivating his players to perform. At a time when most coaches rule with an iron hand or fear, Coach Switzer used positive reinforcement and that made all the difference." – **Keith Jackson, Oklahoma TE, 6X Pro Bowler, Super Bowl Champion, College Football Hall of Famer**

FISHER DEBERRY

"I was a part of Coach DeBerry's first freshmen class when he got the head coaching job at the Air Force Academy. From Day One you could tell he was a man of purpose and passion. He was the ideal person for the unique and challenging position as a coach at a service academy.

His win-loss record speaks for itself, but what truly defines Coach DeBerry is that intangible metric that the majority of his players knew and felt – that he positively cared for them. It's now over 30 years later, and I am still honored to call him 'coach.'" – **Chad Hennings, Air Force DT, Outland Trophy Winner, US Air Force Captain, 3X Super Bowl Champion, College Football Hall of Famer**

PHIL FULMER

"It was an honor and privilege to play for Coach Fulmer. From the first time I met him in December of 1993, when he came to my home, I felt very comfortable talking to him. A significant part of my decision to stay my fourth year was because I wanted to play for Coach Fulmer another year. I learned a lot about football from Coach Fulmer.

Most importantly though, I am thankful for his friendship. The times that we are together on trips, having dinner, playing golf, or hunting are times I truly cherish, and I value his friendship." – **Peyton Manning, Tennessee QB; William V. Campbell Trophy, Maxwell Award Winner; 2X Super Bowl Champion, 5X NFL MVP, NFL All-Time Passing Yards and TD Record Holder, College Football Hall of Famer**

R.C. SLOCUM

"Coach taught me some of the most important virtues as a young man. He taught us to do the right thing all the time and not just some of the time. If you cut corners, more than likely it will catch up to you. He also instilled in me about respecting others. He preached often about the Golden Rule, treat others like you would like to be treated." – **Dat Nguyen, Texas A&M LB; Lombardi, Bednarik, Lambert Trophy Winner; College Football Hall of Famer**

VINCE DOOLEY

"The smartest decision I ever made was to play for Coach Dooley at the University of Georgia. His honesty and integrity exhibited during the recruiting process [when I was] in high school when we met has never wavered. He made no promises, but offered the opportunity to play the game. I would not be in the College Football Hall of Fame if not for Vince Dooley. We aspire to live up to standards of those we admire and respect. His legacy lives in the generations of players that proudly say, 'I played for Coach Vince Dooley.'" – **Scott Woerner, Georgia DB, College Football Hall of Famer**

TERRY DONAHUE

"I give Coach Donahue a lot of credit for my success. He was such a great example for those he coached. He carried himself with class and integrity and always taught us to keep things in the proper perspective. He was tough on me, but he was always honest and I respected that. I became a better player and person because I played for Coach Donahue." – **Troy Aikman, UCLA QB, Davey O'Brien Award Winner, 3X Super Bowl Champion, Super Bowl MVP, 6X Pro Bowler, College and Pro Football Hall of Famer**

FRANK GIRARDI

"Coach Girardi is at the top of my list as far as positive influences in my life. It went well beyond the football field. I always remember the first meeting we had when he became Head Coach and how he stressed loyalty. That was a great message that meant a lot to me. It was more than that, though. He stressed discipline and hard work every day in practice and he rewarded hard work." – **Hon. Thomas I. Vanaskie, Circuit Judge for the United States Court of Appeals for the Third Circuit, Lycoming College DB, All-American**

MARINO CASEM

"I went from being a mediocre student to making the Dean's List twice. I have Coach Casem to thank for that because I really needed someone as demanding as him to grab my attention. Because of his no-nonsense approach, I had to change internally. He made you pay the price if you tried to cut corners. I can honestly say today that I

truly love and respect the man because the pressure he constantly put me under brought greatness out of me. I couldn't have brought that out myself." – **Roynell Young, Alcorn State DB, NFL Pro Bowler**

MIKE BELLOTTI

"Coach Bellotti had a great feel for people. I was always impressed with the staff that he would hire because you could learn as much from all of the assistants as you could from him. He was always genuine, authentic and approachable. You could talk about anything with him, and he made the whole environment a good one. He's a really good guy, not to mention a really good football coach." – **Chris Petersen, Washington Head Coach and former Oregon assistant under Bellotti**

STEVE SPURRIER

"Playing for Coach Spurrier changed the trajectory of my life. He had a combination of two seemingly contradictory qualities: he was the most detail-oriented, somewhat perfectionistic coach I've ever had, and he had an extremely flexible part of himself that would constantly explore better options and make on-the-spot adjustments that would take weeks for other coaches to consider." – **Danny Wuerffel, Florida QB; Heisman Trophy, William V. Campbell Trophy, Maxwell Award, Johnny Unitas Golden Arm Award, Walter Camp Award, Davey O'Brien Award, Sammy Baugh Trophy Winner; College Football Hall of Famer**

Foreword

By Bob Stoops

My life has been shaped by Hall of Fame coaches.

I spent four years playing and five years coaching at Iowa under the great Hayden Fry; coached for seven years as an assistant under the legendary Bill Snyder; was the defensive coordinator for three years under the iconic Steve Spurrier; and just wrapped up 18 years as the Head Coach at the University of Oklahoma, with Barry Switzer living just down the street in Norman.

But I'm also the son of a Hall of Fame high school football coach and that's why I'm passionate about cultivating good coaches.

A good coach doesn't just coach his players for four years and let them go. He is a coach and mentor for life. The most important thing a coach does has nothing to do with teaching a kid how to properly tackle. It's teaching a kid how to be an adult.

I'm proud of what we accomplished on the field during my years of coaching, but I'm most proud when I talk to the young men I coached over a decade ago and see the men they have become. That is why I coached, and it's why my father coached. If you're not into coaching for these reasons, then you're in it for the wrong reasons.

The lessons I learned from my coaching mentors are invaluable. Coach Spurrier's chapter in this book is about how to stand out in coaching. The Ol' Ball Coach's personality and mine are very similar. I learned from him the benefit of coaching "outside the box", and the importance of hiring good assistants.

Coach Spurrier is an offensive genius, and he brought me in to coach up his defense. He was extremely hands-off on defense, trusting me to do my job. On the flip side, when I came to OU, my specialty was defense. But, as I had observed from Coach Spurrier, hiring assistant coaches to balance my strengths was critical. So, I brought in coaches who turned OU into one of the best offensive teams in college football history – guys like Mike Leach, Mark Mangino, Chuck Long, Kevin Wilson, and Lincoln Riley.

Coach Switzer's chapter is about reloading teams instead of rebuilding. Switzer often refers to Oklahoma football as "The Monster" and says the job of the coach is to keep feeding the monster. What he means is this: Oklahoma fans demand success without exception. That was an expectation that Coach Switzer never shied away from, and neither did I. That kind of pressure can get to people, but as Coach Switzer says, "pressure is nothing to worry about." No one puts more pressure on us than we put on ourselves.

Having a work-life balance keeps those things in perspective. Yes, I had to win a bunch of games to keep my job, but at the end of the day, my wife and kids are more important than winning football games.

Now that I've stepped away from coaching, I don't have to reorganize my top priorities, because number one is (and always has been) my family. Oklahoma football goes on without me and that monster is now someone else's to feed. But my family is still with me and that's certainly more important than any win-loss record.

If you're just getting into coaching, this book is a great place to start. If you've been in coaching for a long time, these pages will offer some different perspectives to further your development.

And if you have no interest in coaching at all, you can still learn plenty of life lessons from this book. You may not ever have the need to break down a zone-blocking scheme, but you'll need to be a leader in many different facets of life.

After all, great football coaching is great life coaching.

Introduction

I am so excited for you to read this book. The goal of the National Football Foundation is to promote and develop the power of amateur football in developing the qualities of leadership, sportsmanship, competitive zeal and the drive for academic excellence in America's young people.

I can't think of a better group of men to further this message than these 12 coaches. All of them are highly accomplished on the field and extremely well respected off of it. They represent just a dozen of the thousands of incredible high school and college coaches across the country who dedicate their lives to building up the next generation of young men. We at the NFF truly hope you will benefit from the lessons contained in these pages.

Archie Manning
Chairman, the National Football Foundation &
College Hall of Fame

Winning

CHAPTER 1

Barry Alvarez

HOW TO BUILD A WINNING CULTURE

"I made sure that anyone that touched the program understood what was expected of them and how we wanted our program to run. I didn't care if it was trainers or someone in the equipment room or the cafeteria; if they dealt with my athletes, I wanted them to know exactly what I expected from them, and I wanted a commitment from them. Everyone knew their responsibilities and were held accountable, just like the players."

When Notre Dame Defensive Coordinator Barry Alvarez took the Head Coach position for the Wisconsin Badgers in 1989, the differences between his former home and his future one couldn't have been more profound.

Alvarez was leaving what could arguably be considered the most historic program in college football, one that claimed 11 national titles, including 1988's undefeated season under Coach Lou Holtz. The Fighting Irish were, and still are, a consistent moneymaker, always selling out their stadium.

In contrast, Alvarez headed to a Badger program saddled with millions of dollars in debt, a half-empty stadium, and, most significantly, a culture of losing football. In the 100-year history of Wisconsin football before Alvarez, the team had won zero Rose Bowls, hadn't won a conference title since 1962, and had finished a season ranked in the AP Poll only four times since 1962.

Photo courtesy of Dave Stluka/Wisconsin Athletics.

Alvarez had his work cut out for him, and it didn't come easy. After a debut season that finished 1-10, the Badgers followed that up with two 5-6 seasons. Both were improvements, but Alvarez and his players didn't put it all together until 1993, when the Badgers finished the season 10-1-1 and defeated UCLA in the 1994 Rose Bowl.

In Alvarez's 16 seasons in charge, Wisconsin won the Rose Bowl three times, the Big Ten three times, and he had a Heisman Trophy winner with Ron Dayne.

Alvarez is currently the Director of Athletics at Wisconsin, a role that has enabled him to make sure that the winning culture he brought to Madison continues. His successor, Bret Bielema, took Wisconsin to three more

Rose Bowls, while current coach Paul Chryst won the Cotton Bowl in his second season in charge.

Alvarez, who grew up in Langeloth, Pennsylvania, played linebacker at Nebraska under coach Bob Devaney. He coached high school football for Lexington High School in Nebraska and Mason City High School in Iowa, where he won the 1978 4A state title. He then moved into the college ranks, becoming the linebackers coach at Iowa and then Notre Dame, where he was promoted to defensive coordinator for the 1988 national championship season.

Everywhere Alvarez coached, success followed. He was inducted into the College Football Hall of Fame in 2010.

What made you want to go into coaching?

I come from a small mining community in western Pennsylvania where athletics was important. It was a blue-collar area where families followed and supported athletics. Growing up, we had very good youth athletic programs.

I happened to be good at football and had some very influential and talented coaches that coached me from a young age all the way through high school. I took to sport. Once I got to college on a scholarship, I realized that this was what I wanted to do for a living. I wanted to be like Bob Devaney.

Coaches Who Influenced Me

High School: Pat McGraw

College: Bob Devaney (CFB Hall Class of 1981)

Colleagues: Hayden Fry (CFB Hall 2003), Lou Holtz (CFB Hall 2008), Monte Kiffin, Tom Osborne (CFB Hall 1999)

What did these coaches have in common?

They were all good communicators. They had a passion for the game, and they cared for players.

What was your favorite part about being a coach?

Working with, teaching, and developing players.

What was the hardest part?

Losing.

What is the No. 1 piece of advice you give a young coach?

I tell a young coach: Be in coaching for the right reasons. You're in coaching to help develop young people. Don't ever lose track of that. Give your full attention to those players that you're working with. Care about them as people, not just players.

Don't worry about your next job. Do as good a job as you can where you are. Others will notice.

Do you think that many coaches these days have lost sight of those ideals?

The money is getting so big now. I see some coaches that are more worried about the next job than their current job. I see more of that now than I saw in the past. The salaries have a lot to do with that.

As Director of Athletics, how do you make sure the coaches you hire aren't already looking for the next job?

You try to feel that out in visiting with him so that you can read between the lines. You do your due diligence. You talk to people that have played for him and people that have coached with him to find out what type of person he is, what he hangs his hat on, and whether he cares about kids.

Why does football matter?

I think football is a microcosm of life. It teaches so many life lessons – teamwork and dealing with adversity, setting goals and reaching goals with a group. The values and things you learn in football carry over into life.

HOW TO BUILD A WINNING CULTURE

You had success everywhere you coached, whether it was in high school, as an assistant, or as a Head Coach at Wisconsin. What were some traits that helped make you successful?

I had a passion for coaching, and it was important to me. The players that played for me felt that. I had a passion for my athletes and for taking care of them. They all felt that I did care about them as a person and that whatever I asked them to do wasn't unfair because they knew that I cared for them. They knew that I was committed, and I was able to get a commitment from them.

What are some adjustments you made as you gained experience?

You adjust how you practice. You learn from that. You're a little more sensitive to your athletes' needs. As I grew older and more experienced, I was able to read my athletes more and really know what they needed, whether that was a longer or shorter practice, or less or more contact. As I gained experience, I felt I had a very strong sense of that.

You came into a program that had never had any sustained success. How did you set the tone on Day One to help change the culture at Wisconsin?

I made sure that anyone that touched the program understood what was expected of them and how we wanted our program to run. I didn't care if it was trainers or someone in the equipment room or the cafeteria; if they dealt with my athletes, I wanted them to know exactly what I expected from them, and I wanted a commitment from them. Everyone knew their responsibilities and were held accountable, just like the players.

Changing the culture didn't happen overnight. Your first season was 1-10. How tough was it to continue to stick to the plan and believe in yourself and your team as the losses piled up?

That was the first losing season I'd had for a long time. We just didn't have the players. Our guys played hard, but we couldn't move the ball. We had a good defense. The last game of the year we played a very good Michigan State team, and we dropped a pass in the end zone to lose the game. It was 14-9. Our guys had played hard.

It was then that I knew I had the players. I knew the guys were committed. The guys understood what we were selling, and the guys bought into it. That was what motivated me in the off-season to keep doing what we were doing. I knew we were going to improve with the kids we recruited. You have to look for different things, and it's not wins – it's improvement. You want to see improvement, and you want people in the program to buy in.

The next year we only won five games. Our guys didn't quite know how to win yet. There were probably three or four more games that we probably could have won.

Is there a way to teach players how to win?

Sometimes somebody just has to make a play to get over the hump. There's no magical formula to teach somebody how to win. It's how you practice. It's the expectations you have. It's the little things that you're coaching every day that sooner or later will sink in.

And it all paid off with a 10-1-1 season in 1993 and a win in the 1994 Rose Bowl over UCLA. What did it feel like to finally get over the hump and do it in such a major way?

That's really special. When you've got a staff and players that committed themselves three years earlier, and for three years put so much into it and came so close, and then all of a sudden you get over the hump. You know going into the season that you're good enough to compete with anyone. To see it play out – and not only go to the Rose Bowl, but win the Rose Bowl – that's what this business is all about. It makes all the hard work and sacrifice that you've gone through all worth it.

A lot of teams have random years of success and then fall off quickly, but Wisconsin has been a Big

Ten and national power since that 1994 Rose Bowl. What are some specific strategies that you employed to keep that winning culture in Madison?

It's constantly trying to improve. Not being satisfied with where you are. Understanding who you are and how you win in a specific place. We're in the Midwest, we're not a populated state, and we don't have an overabundance of players in Wisconsin. We probably have five to eight players offered in our state every year. I call us a developmental program. We can consistently recruit linemen here in our state – occasionally we'll get good skill players – but every year we're going to get good linemen, big kids.

I felt we could build a good walk-on program that could give us an advantage. Other schools weren't using it. I would actively recruit 20 walk-ons a year and maybe five would end up being scholarship players. Those guys ended up being leaders for us. They set a tone for the attitude that we wanted.

It's been over two decades since that first Rose Bowl victory. There are generations of kids that only know of Wisconsin as a perennial power. It's been over a decade since you were Head Coach. What have your successors done to make sure the winning culture didn't end with your tenure?

I was talking to a group of young people recently about when we came in and how we turned the program around. I said, "How many of you were born after 1990?" Many of their hands went up. They didn't know that Wisconsin used to be bad!

I've gone through three different coaches as Director of Athletics. I hired Bret Bielema; he had been my assistant, so he knew the formula. After Bret left, we started to drift away from the formula, and we were losing our edge. So I then brought back Paul Chryst, who grew up in Madison, played for the Badgers, and was an assistant for both me and Bret. He knew our formula for success, and it's worked for him in his first two years.

With the success that you had as a coach, did you find that recruiting became easier? Did you ever change your strategy as the team's profile got bigger?

We had the 1999 Heisman Trophy winner with Ron Dayne, and I figured every high school running back in the country would want to come here. I would bring the top RBs in from across the country, but it was hard to land those guys. We would come in second because they would want to stay close to home, or they would want to go to a school with a sexier name. We learned to stick with the type of kid we were going to get, the areas where we are established and the relationships with the coaches that trust us. We learned to stick with what we know.

We recruited kids that knew this was a developmental program: we're going to teach you how to play, and the off-season is going to be very difficult. They came here because they felt they could have success. If you come here, you have a good chance of being in a bowl game every year. Kids want to go somewhere they can be successful.

Barry Alvarez Career Stats

Career Record – 119-74-4

Conference Titles – 3

Consensus All-Americans – 9

Heisman Trophy Winners – 1 (Ron Dayne 1999)

Bobby Dodd, AFCA, College & Pro Football Weekly National Coach of the Year Winner – 1993

Victor Award Winner – 2001

College Football Hall of Fame – 2010

CHAPTER 2

Tom Osborne

HOW TO WIN CONSISTENTLY

"We tried to be positive. I felt that the best way to change behavior was to catch somebody doing something right and reinforce that. We never wanted players to be humiliated or made fun of for something personal. Certainly you had to correct players, but we did it in the right way. Above all, the players knew we cared about them as people."

Tom Osborne capped off 25 incredibly successful years as Head Coach of the Nebraska Cornhuskers with perhaps the greatest walk-off in coaching history. His last five seasons, the Cornhuskers were 60-3 and won three national titles in four years.

Osborne's 1995 team, led by superstar quarterback Tommie Frazier, is widely regarded as the greatest college football team ever.

But Osborne's career isn't just about those final five years. His consistency as a Head Coach for 25 years is stunning: He never won fewer than nine games. He never lost more than three games.

In addition, he won 13 conference titles. In fact, if it wasn't for Barry Switzer's Oklahoma teams, Osborne would have won even more conference and (possibly) national titles as Switzer beat Osborne 12 times. A full 25 percent of Osborne's career losses were to Oklahoma, mostly in the 1970s. Conversely, Osborne handed Switzer five of his 29 career losses, accounting for 20 percent of his defeats.

Photo courtesy of Nebraska Athletics.

By the time the mid-1990s came around, however, Osborne essentially could not be beaten. His 1995 team averaged a 38.6-point margin of victory, including a 62-24 Fiesta Bowl victory against Florida – still the largest margin of victory in a national championship game.

Following his complete domination of college football, Osborne retired after the 1997 season. Eventually, he would be elected to three terms as a United States Congressman, serving until 2007. He then took on the role of Nebraska's Athletics Director from 2007–2013. Osborne was inducted into the College Football Hall of Fame as a coach in 1999.

What made you want to go into coaching?

Really, I wasn't very intentional about it. I played college football as a quarterback at Hastings. I spent three years in the NFL, then had an injury and couldn't play anymore. I came back to graduate school with the intention of going into college administration work. Athletics had been such a huge part of my life up until that point at age 25, but I thought it was time to ease my way out of it.

Bob Devaney had just been hired as the Nebraska Head Coach, so I asked him if I could serve as a graduate assistant coach. I thought I would do that for a couple of years and get athletics out of my system. One thing led to another, and I continued in graduate school.

It eventually came to a point where I had to make a decision. I was getting pressure from football to go full-time and pressure from graduate school to take on students and serve as an academic advisor. I finally just felt the pull of coaching – it was too strong – so I asked Bob if he would hire me full-time, and he did. One thing led to another, and I just never got out of coaching.

I stayed with it roughly 36 years. I don't regret that decision at all. I enjoyed my time in coaching very much.

Coaches Who Influenced Me

Childhood – Charles Osborne (father)

College – Tom McLaughlin

Colleagues – Bob Devaney (CFB Hall 1981)

What were some of the characteristics of these coaches that you liked?

Tom McLaughlin was the coach at Hastings College, and he was typical of many coaches years ago who did it all. He made sure the field was lined before the game; he coached football, basketball, and track. I admired what he was able to do with such limited resources.

Bob Devaney was such a people person. He had a good sense of humor, and even though he had a temper, he never stayed mad. We were very different, but I learned a lot from him and the way he handled players.

What was your favorite part of being a coach?

I really enjoyed the interaction with players and watching them grow and develop as players and as people. One of the most satisfying things about coaching is that those relationships continue. Hardly a day goes by that I don't have some kind of interaction with a former player. That's been one of the very nice things about coaching.

What's the hardest part about being a coach?

I took over Nebraska in 1973, and we had won a national championship in 1970 and 1971. So the bar was set very high. It was a situation where the only good year was a national championship – it was difficult. I loved Nebraska and I wanted to coach here, but I also knew that following someone like Bob Devaney and his success was difficult to do. Most people that follow legendary coaches don't last very long. I had an interview at Texas Tech and almost got that job (and was in the running for several others), but I decided to stay at Nebraska. I thought that if I was able to last five years at Nebraska, then that would be pretty good.

We had a tough time with Oklahoma early on. They were really good – and we were good, too – but not as good as Oklahoma. So a 9-3 or a 10-2 season didn't measure up in the eyes of Husker fans. That was difficult to live with, but I did manage to get out of that early period and turn the corner and have some really good teams later on.

What is your No. 1 piece of advice that you would give to a young coach?

You have to be pretty well grounded philosophically. It's important that you understand yourself and your strengths and weakness. It's important that you really know your craft. You have to be really diligent and study the game. There are lots of ways to coach successfully, and there are many different styles of coaching – different offenses, defenses, and special teams.

You have to decide what you believe in. You're going to get all kinds of people pushing you and pulling you to make changes. They'll tell you to throw the ball more, or run the ball more, or do this or do that. You're not going to be able to please everybody. You can't be pushed to the "flavor of the week" when it comes to your offense and your defense. You have to understand who you are and which coaching system is best for you.

It's really important that you care about your players and put their welfare first. If they feel that from you, then sometimes you can ask very difficult things of them and they'll respond because they know that what you're asking them to do is making them a better player. Caring about your players is very fundamental.

Why does football matter to you?

Football combines a lot of the elements that are basic to American character – particularly, the frontier society. Vince Lombardi once said that football is a Spartan game, and it really is. It's a very physical game. There's a certain amount of risk involved. It's certainly a team game because all 11 offensive and defensive players have to work as a unit. If everyone isn't doing their task, then things break down. It's the ultimate team game.

In football you can do a lot to develop as a player. In the off-season strength-and-training program, you can take a player with average talent and work on strength, speed, and agility, and you can turn that player into a pretty good football player.

But it takes time. In some other sports, athletic ability carries you further faster. For example, in basketball you see a number of college freshmen make a great impact on a team, whereas it's more unusual for a true freshman to make the same impact on a football team.

Of course, attitude and mind-set are really important. In football you have to be aggressive yet disciplined in your approach to the game.

HOW TO WIN CONSISTENTLY

You followed up the legendary Bob Devaney. Did you focus on continuing everything he did, or did you want to differentiate yourself?

It's important that each coach be himself. I could not be Bob Devaney. He was a gregarious Irishman. He had a great sense of humor and was a very good storyteller. That wasn't me. Eventually I did develop some of those traits, but that wasn't who I was. I had to be myself. So, for fans and players, it was a contrast. I was this young guy who was pretty focused and who had a very different sense of humor. This contrast, plus not being able to beat Oklahoma for the first five years, was something that the fans and players weren't very excited about.

You can't try to be somebody other than yourself. As time went on, we began to win a little bit more. We never really had a bad team, and I think our preparation was good. We continued to feel that physical football, running the ball well, and stopping the run were pretty basic to what we were doing. And we had good discipline on our teams.

Nebraska, like all schools, comes with its challenges and advantages. How did you find the formula for success?

In coaching you always change and evolve. Some changes depend on personnel. If you have a quarterback who's a good runner, then you want to maximize those running abilities. If a guy's a better passer, then you throw the ball more. You always innovate. You look to do something that people haven't seen before. If you run the exact same offense and defense that most of the schools in your conference are running, then you better have superior personnel because you're not going to have much of a surprise element. There's no question that over 25 years as a Head Coach, I did evolve and change.

One of the great lessons that we learned was that speed and athleticism at quarterback were very important. We had QBs early on that were more NFL-type guys – good throwers, but not great runners. We were having trouble with Oklahoma, and they had a lot of speed and athleticism at QB. We had some close games where it came down to a QB scrambling and picking up a first down or buying some time to make a big play. So we eventually evolved to an option-type game, with a QB that could hurt you with a run or a pass. We didn't go to the wishbone; we stuck with the I-formation because we believed that if we had one great running back that we could put at the top of the "I," where he could run any place on the field, then we'd be successful. We learned a lot from Oklahoma.

The other thing we noticed was that Oklahoma was more difficult than any other team to defend because they ran the wishbone. No one else in the conference was running that, so it made it hard to prepare for them because they were doing something entirely different. You only had four days of practice to prepare for it. So we realized we ought to do something different and not just be like everybody else. We wanted to be that changeup so when somebody hit Nebraska, they wouldn't see the same offense that they saw from other teams.

What was something that you did from Day One that you carried through until your last day coaching?

No. 1, we had a sense of identity. We wanted to be very physical. I didn't allow my QBs to run out-of-bounds or slide. We wanted all the players on the team to understand that the quarterback was a football player, and he would be as physical as all the other players. We expected them to run the ball and sometimes block. Receivers had to block every play downfield. We ran a lot of different formations and plays, but most people that played us would say that we were very physical, both offensively and defensively, so we knew if we had an identity and stayed true to that, we'd be successful.

We were also consistent. If we lost a game, we didn't come back to Nebraska and practice until two in the morning. We didn't extend practice if we had a bad game. We always stayed with the same routine. The players knew what to expect.

In terms of my disposition, I was fairly even-keeled and didn't fly off the handle. I wasn't a volatile guy where the players didn't know which Head Coach would show up on a given day. My faith was very important to me, and I stayed anchored to that. I didn't impose my faith on any of my players, but I also let them know that the spiritual dimension was just as important as the physical and intellectual dimensions. We made that available to our players in terms of chapel and mass on the mornings of games. I think over time there was a fairly strong spiritual dimension amongst our team.

Integrity was very important. We made sure that if we told a player that he was going to get in the game in the second quarter, he would actually play in the second quarter, and if we told a player that if he got stronger and faster, then we'd let him compete for a starting job, we tried to make sure that was true.

We never offered anyone anything that was illegal. We tried to be positive, too. I felt that the best way to change behavior was to catch somebody doing something right and reinforce that. We never wanted players to be humiliated or made fun of for something personal. Certainly you had to correct players, but we did it in the right way.

Above all, the players knew we cared about them as people.

Unlike many coaches, your best years were at the end. Was there something that you figured out that worked best in those years, or was it just down to having the most talented players that you'd had in your time?

I think it was a combination of things. In 1991, we found a new low point. We were 9-3 that year. Two of the games we lost were close games to Colorado, and then we also lost to Georgia Tech in our bowl game. We lost our QB toward the end of the season. We were 9-3 and didn't feel like we played as well as we could have, so we evaluated everything.

We established something called the Unity Council where we had players selected from each segment of the team: two offensive linemen, defensive linemen, running backs, and on and on. We had 16 players on the council, and we wanted them to meet up once a week and talk about anything that they knew of that was getting in the way of team unity. They would then bring those issues to me.

It might have been something simple like they didn't like the way we played certain games or something we were doing in practice. We addressed the minor issues, and the players felt like we were listening to them and hearing them.

One thing we always valued was the process. John Wooden, the great UCLA basketball coach, never talked about winning. He never talked about end results. He would talk about how to put your socks on so you don't get blisters, how to get in a defensive stance, how to bend your knees on a free throw. His theory was that if you practiced the right things well enough and often enough, then winning would take care of itself.

So we established our own set of goals, which kind of broke the game down. We wanted no turnovers on offense, three takeaways on defense, six yards per rush on offense, and on and on. We evaluated our performance on Monday. We talked with the players about how we did in each phase of the game. If we hit nine of our 12 goals on offense, eight or nine out of the 11 goals on defense, and five or six of our seven goals on special teams, then we played well. We might have lost the game, but we played well. On the other hand, if we won by 40 points but we didn't meet our goals, then we didn't play well.

So it was a continual emphasis on the process – how we did on Monday and Tuesday and Wednesday and Thursday. We never talked about winning, but we did talk about how we could come as close as possible to the perfect game.

Bobby Knight said that the goal is the perfect game, but you're probably never going to play it. Still, you try to come as close as you can.

What would retiring Tom Osborne say to Tom Osborne on the first day of his head-coaching career?

There's always a certain evolution in a coaching career. For example, it's important for a Head Coach not to get too far from the game. It's easy to become the CEO-type coach where the coordinators do everything and you become a spectator. But when things go south on you during a game, it's important to be engaged enough and knowledgeable enough to make adjustments and decisions.

For me, I was always engaged with the offense. However, I was always in touch with the defense. I watched every snap of the preseason defensive plays. But it's impossible for one person to be tremendously detail-oriented in multiple phases of the game. So I had to find the balance between being the CEO-type and being too far from the game versus being too detail-oriented and focused on every facet.

I think over time I became more people-oriented and maybe not quite as driven. Part of it was the nature of the expectations when I took over. I began to focus on trying to win games to keep my job for the next year, but as time went on, I began to focus more on the process and the people. But I wouldn't say that those things weren't important to me in 1973. It was probably more of an evolutionary process.

Tom Osborne Career Stats

Career Record – 255-49-3

National Championships – 3

Conference Titles – 13

Consensus All-Americans – 25

Heisman Trophy Winners – 1 (Mike Rozier 1983)

Bobby Dodd Coach of the Year – 1978

AFCA National Coach of the Year – 1994

National Football Foundation Distinguished American Award – 1995

ESPN Coach of the Decade – 1999

College Football Hall of Fame – 1999

CHAPTER 3

Barry Switzer

HOW TO RELOAD

"I had players who believed in me and believed in how we treated them. They sold me and the program to others. Players will tell recruits the truth. Your players have more to do with selling the program than any coach."

It wasn't until Barry Switzer's 30th game in charge of the Oklahoma Sooners that he lost a game. That's almost three full seasons!

Switzer's career winning percentage of .837 is ranked third amongst all retired major conference FBS coaches. Only legends Knute Rockne and Frank Leahy rank ahead of him, and he ranks ahead of former Nebraska coach and contemporary Tom Osborne by .001 percentage point. (If Switzer is aware of this last fact, you'd better believe he's brought it up to Osborne at the many dinners and events at which they find themselves together these days.)

Switzer is a one-of-a-kind personality who coached a wildly successful Oklahoma Sooners squad from 1973-1988. During the 1970s, he lost only seven games in eight seasons. Although he won three national titles, he also had years of 10-0-1 and 11-1 (four separate times) that did not result in national titles.

Switzer with former players Jack Mildren and Roy Bell. Photo courtesy of Oklahoma Athletics.

Even with this record, he did have some "down" years in charge. Between 1981 and 1983, the Sooners lost four games each year. The 12 losses in those three years would account for almost half his total career losses. It's definitely worth noting that losing only four games during a season would get coaches at most schools a raise – especially when the losses from those years are examined. The 1981 season featured losses to the No. 1, No. 3, and No. 5 teams; in 1982 they lost to No. 18, No. 3, and No. 11; and in 1983 to No. 6, No. 2, and No. 1.

In retrospect, these were far from "down" years. But the demanding Sooner faithful doesn't care how other schools would feel about these seasons. To them, they were disappointments. Switzer had to start improving –

and fast. So he took the team to four straight Orange Bowls, winning the 1985 national championship in the process. It was exactly the kind of response Sooner fans were looking for.

The saying goes that schools like Oklahoma don't ever rebuild; they reload. Switzer was an expert at reloading, year after year.

When he left Oklahoma, Switzer went on to coach the Dallas Cowboys to the Super Bowl XXX title, becoming one of three Head Coaches to win a college football national title and the Super Bowl. He played center and linebacker for College Football Hall of Famer Frank Broyles at Arkansas and was inducted into the CFB Hall as a coach in 2001.

What made you want to go into coaching?

Bob Stoops, who was here longer as the Head Coach than I was, often says that he knew that he was going to be a coach when he was growing up as a young lad because his dad was a coach. That influenced all the Stoops boys, who are all coaches.

Well, people often ask me how I was inspired to be a coach, and I say, "Well, it damn sure wasn't by my daddy being a coach. My daddy was a bootlegger, and I damn sure didn't want to end up in the state penitentiary like he did." So I damn sure wasn't going to be a bootlegger.

When I went to college, I was like most of the kids that I would eventually recruit. I was a 17-year-old as a freshman. I was too young. I damn sure hadn't thought about what the hell I wanted to do in life. I didn't have a desire to be a coach at the time. When I got to college, they stuck me in physical education classes – I think they stuck every football player in that major. I didn't like it.

After a year, I transferred to business school and got my business degree. I've often thought about it, and I probably would have gotten into business with Sam Walton. I knew him, and he was just getting started with Walmart at that time. I also went to school with Don Tyson of Tyson Poultry, so I really thought about getting into business. But first, I went into the Army and served my country.

When I got out, I went back to Arkansas to go to law school. My brother's an attorney and so were two of my uncles. Since I'd played football at Arkansas and I'd coached the freshman team for one year before the Army, Frank Broyles gave me a call and asked me what my plans were. (I was his captain when we won his first Southwest Conference championship.) I told him I was going to law school, and he said, "I'd like for you to coach, scout, and recruit for me. I want you to live in the dorms and be my dorm coach." He told me that if I didn't like it, I could go to law school the next year. I spent four decades in coaching, so I obviously liked it.

I got involved at the collegiate level, and I was very fortunate that I had a coach like Frank Broyles that believed in me. I got to be associated with a lot of good assistant coaches at Arkansas, and then, after 13 years as an assistant, I got the opportunity to be the Head Coach of Oklahoma. It was something I never intended or planned for. It was a second thought, but I enjoyed it.

I learned to love it because of the great influence you have on young people's lives. When you recruit a player, you've got them for life. You end up knowing more about them than a lot of their parents. You know their passions, goals, and desires. They're an extension of your family. I believe that my relationship that I had with my players was one of the reasons I was successful as a coach. I contribute all my success to my players and assistant coaches.

.

Coaches Who Influenced Me

High School – Lynn Yarbrough, Harry Denson

College – Frank Broyles (CFB Hall 1983)

Colleagues – Hayden Fry (CFB Hall 2003), Doug Dickey (CFB Hall 2003), Jim Mackenzie, Bill Pace, Johnny Majors, Merv Johnson, and all my assistant coaches at OU

How did these coaches help mold and shape you?

When I was going to high school, I lived out in the country, and not many people had cars in the late 1940s. I quit football in eighth grade because I didn't like walking home on that gravel road when it was dark at night. A few days after I quit, a man named Lynn Yarbrough, who was the Athletics Director at the high school and the former football coach there, came to me and asked me why I quit. I told him why, and he offered to have some men around the town take turns driving me home after practice. If he hadn't taken an interest in me, I might not have played football again.

What was your favorite part of coaching?

Winning and winning! That's the best part.

No, really it was the relationships with the coaches and players. I have a lot of championships, but when I look back, the things that are really important to me are not all those wins but the players and the relationships.

What was the hardest part of coaching?

There's a hell of a lot of hard parts. The worst thing to me was telling a kid that he couldn't come to Oklahoma even though he wanted to play for us. I had so many kids from this state that wanted to play for Oklahoma, and having to tell a kid that I didn't think he could play at this level was hard. I would tell them that they should prove me wrong at another school, and a lot of them did when they played for our competition. Telling them no ... that was tough to do.

And, obviously there comes a time when you have to make tough decisions that affect young men's lives. I've had to ask people to leave our program for disciplinary reasons. That's always tough to do.

I'm a guy that likes to give second chances. You never read about the kids who take advantage of their second chances. There are a lot more of those than the unsuccessful ones. You always hear about the ones that don't take advantage of it, and they make a bad choice again. Then the media beats your ass up because you ought to have known not to give him a second chance. I'd always point out that they didn't hear about all the second chances that were successful.

What's your No. 1 piece of advice that you give to young coaches?

You got to start at the bottom. Even if you played the game, you have to start at the bottom and work your way up.

Why does football matter?

There's great lessons in football. I don't know how many kids out there know what mental and physical toughness is. If you didn't play a team sport, I don't

know if you understand what self-sacrifice means, what
it means to pay a price to be a team member.

I remember going to spring practice thinking about
everyone else on campus taking blankets and cases of
beer down to the lake with sorority girls while I was over
there busting my ass, sprinting for two hours on the practice field. You learn a lot of intangibles as a team member that help you in life. Team sports do that for you.
You learn self-discipline. You learn the willingness to
prepare. Everyone wants to win, but are they willing to
prepare to win? These things are what team sports do for
you. Kids learn to make this a part of their personality. It
becomes second nature. It becomes the only way you
know to do things. It carries over to everything you do in
life. That's what team sports do. If you've never been
part of team sports, then you might not understand these
things.

The one thing I've always heard people say is that
sports build character. That's bull. Sports don't build
character. They build all those intangibles that I talked
about – diversity, teamwork. All those things are great
and will help you in living your life. But character?
Character is doing the right thing when no one is around.
On the field, everyone is watching. You build character
when no one is around. You learn it in your formative
years. It's a value system that separates you from a lot of
people.

If you've never played competitive sports, then I think you're behind.

HOW TO RELOAD

You had an incredible start to your head-coaching career, and you maintained that success throughout your career. How did you take that initial success and make it last?

I had a great product to sell, the University of Oklahoma. I didn't build the tradition here – Bud Wilkinson did. I continued to add to it. I call it "feeding the monster." When I coached in the '70s, only two schools won over 100 games in that decade. We were one of them; the other was Alabama. I had some good coaches to sell the product, but most importantly I had players who believed in me and in how we treated them. They sold me and the program to others. Players will tell recruits the truth. Your players have more to do with selling the program than any coach. I was able to attract good players, and they were happy and believed in me and my coaches. Good things were happening.

Even though by most standards your 1981–1983 seasons were successful, by Oklahoma standards those teams struggled a bit. What happened in those years, and how did you recover so quickly?

I got away from the wishbone. I had dropped off a bit talent-wise. I was able to recruit and get it back and get back to the philosophy I believed in. I changed to the I-formation for Marcus Dupree, but then he left our program. When that happened, I struggled a little bit to get back, but it didn't take me long to get back to kicking Texas and Nebraska's ass and winning Big Eight championships and then a national championship in 1985.

When you say "struggled," we won eight games and only lost to the good teams that were better than us – Texas, Ohio State, USC, Nebraska. There's no shame in losing to great teams with great traditions.

You talk about "feeding the monster" at Oklahoma. Coaching at a winning school like that comes with a lot of pressure. Did that ever get to you?

I never thought about pressure. I knew what we could do. Our coaches just did what we had to do, and if it wasn't good enough, then we would have been gone. But it was obviously good enough. The year I resigned we won nine games.

I never worried about pressure. I laughed about it. What the hell is pressure? Pressure is when the doctor tells you or a family member that you've got a certain amount of time to live. That's pressure. But winning football games? They can't execute you if you lose a few. At least I don't think they can.

Wade Phillips had a great line. He said he would be worried if they only fired bad coaches. But they fire good coaches all the time too, so there's no reason to worry!

I always loved that line.

Barry Switzer Career Stats

Career Record – 157-29-4

National Championships – 3

Conference Titles – 12

Consensus All-Americans – 22

Heisman Trophy Winners – 1 (Billy Sims 1978)

Sporting News Coach of the Year – 1973

Walter Camp Coach of the Year – 1974

Super Bowl XXX Champion

College Football Hall of Fame – 2001

CHAPTER 4

Fisher DeBerry

HOW TO PICK THE RIGHT SYSTEM

"You have got to believe in what you're doing as a coach and approach it with a very, very positive attitude. Then your kids will get on board."

In the modern era of college football, winning at a service academy – be it Army, Navy, or Air Force – is extremely difficult. Army and Navy often dominated college football in the first half of the 20th century, with the Black Knights claiming three national championships in the 1940s and the Midshipmen claiming one in 1926. But since Fisher DeBerry became Head Coach at Air Force in 1984, taking over the reins from Ken Hatfield, the Falcons have been the template for success when it comes to service-academy football.

Numerous factors led to the decline of service-academy football, but the bottom line was that by 1984, the academies no longer got the best athletes. Something needed to change in order to compete. The academies needed to think differently than the rest of the teams in the country. Coach Hatfield and his assistants, including Coach DeBerry, decided to run the triple option, which meant that the lack of size on the offensive line was less glaring. It meant opposing teams would be unprepared for an unorthodox offense. And, most importantly, it meant that Air Force could recruit athletes that didn't interest other schools.

Photo courtesy Air Force Athletics.

This change took Hatfield and DeBerry from a 2-9 record in Hatfield's first year to a 10-2 record in his fifth and final year. After Hatfield returned to Arkansas, his alma mater, DeBerry remained as the Falcons' Head Coach and took them to soaring heights in his 23 years in that position. His teams had 17 winning seasons and played in 12 bowl games. They also won the Commander-in-Chief's Trophy, given to the service academy with the best record against the other two each year, 14 times and tied for it once. As the winningest coach in service-academy history, his crowning season was the 1985 season in which the Falcons went 12-1 and beat Texas in the Bluebonnet Bowl. Only a seven-point loss to BYU kept them from competing for a national championship.

Perhaps the greatest measure of the impact that De-Berry has had on college football is the fact that all three service academies follow the blueprint DeBerry laid down at Air Force by running a version of the triple option.

DeBerry, who now lives in Isle of Palms, South Carolina, grew up in Cheraw, South Carolina, and played football and baseball at Wofford College. He was inducted into the College Football Hall of Fame in 2011.

What made you want to go into coaching?

I've always had a real interest in people. I just feel so grateful that some people showed some interest in me. I grew up in a small community in Cheraw, South Carolina. The people there gave me a lot of encouragement and showed a lot of interest in me. My high school and college coaches had a tremendous impact on my life.

I was the product of a single-parent household, and I never really had a father figure in my life. I lived with my grandparents, but my granddad and my mother worked a lot. My grandmother was the one who really watched after me.

We were blessed to have lived almost right in the middle of town, right across the street from the high school football and baseball fields. I've been told I was over at those fields from the time I was able to walk, even when I was in diapers with a bottle of milk in my pocket. I had nowhere else to go. My grandparents and my mom knew where I was.

I was constantly playing some form of ball all year long. That was about all that I could do. That was basically all the entertainment we had. On Saturday, we would get up early to get to the field so we could get picked for a team. We would play until lunchtime, then maybe go to a movie (which cost us 9 cents), and then come back and play until dark.

I was blessed to have some good coaches in high school. I guess I was a decent player, but when I got to Wofford College, my coaches really embraced me. I played for a man named Jim Brakefield, who was the defensive coordinator and the baseball coach. I played baseball and football. I wasn't a great player, but I hustled and worked hard.

I must have made an impression on him because after I got out of the Army and coached for five years in high school, Coach Brakefield asked me to come to Wofford to be the secondary coach. Of course, at the time you only had about five coaches on staff.

We were blessed at Wofford. We won 21 games in a row and played in the National Small College Championship. From there, Coach Brakefield went to Appalachian State University and asked me to come with him as his first assistant. I coached defense for about five years and then offense for six years.

Who are the coaches you leaned on when you became a Head Coach?

When I became a Head Coach, the first person I called was Bobby Bowden and I said, "What the heck do I do?" He said, "Why don't you just come down here?" So I did, and I stayed with him for three or four days. The next guy I called was Grant Teaff, and I stayed with him for three or four days. I learned a lot from those guys.

How did you end up at Air Force?

Ken Hatfield and I had become very good friends through the Fellowship of Christian Athletes. He was coaching at Tennessee, and then he went to Florida with Doug Dickey. They were running some option, and at Appalachian State we were running the wishbone. That was one of the things that really helped my career – that we were running the wishbone at Wofford, ahead of a lot of schools. We sort of got on the forefront and went to Appalachian, who was transitioning to the Southern Conference. We had some wins over much bigger programs.

When Coach Hatfield became Air Force Head Coach after Bill Parcells' one year there, he realized they didn't have a lot of offensive continuity or a plan, so he decided on the triple option. He hired me in order to do something different. Everybody in the West was throwing the football; the triple option was unique and innovative at the time. We won two games, then four games, then eight, and then ten games. Ken had always said he would only leave the academy for his alma mater of Arkansas or for Missouri. Sure enough, Coach Frank Broyles gave him a call and asked him to come to Arkansas.

Rather than following Coach Hatfield to Arkansas, I was asked to stay at the Academy. Those kids had worked so hard and had made such a commitment to what we were doing, I just felt like it was a good opportunity to stay with them. And that's where I ended up for 23 years. I wouldn't trade it for anything in the world.

What is the No. 1 piece of advice that you would give a young coach?

You've got to have a reason why you're doing what you do. That's what makes you committed. So many coaches today tend to think that they can make a little bit more money somewhere else, or want to jump to a bigger program. But coaching is coaching no matter what level you're coaching. You've got to have a reason that you want to coach.

My whole reason for coaching was to give back. So many people had given to me and had impacted my life. I always felt that since certain people took such an interest in me, if I could take the same interest and convey my beliefs to others, then it would be rewarding. That's what I think coaching is all about.

One thing that really motivated me was that my coaches at Wofford let me coach at the local high school, and I was able to help many of the players that I'd been playing with a few years before. That inspired me because I saw a little bit of what coaching would be like.

I was never interested in coaching for the money. I just wanted to help somebody like my coaches had helped me. That's what my wife and I are doing today. We're managing a foundation that we started in 2002. As I traveled around, I saw so many kids in single-parent families. Each year I saw more and more kids that had been denied opportunities because maybe their mom couldn't afford it. Today, 42 percent of kids live in single-parent families. Having grown up in a single-parent family, I never felt I was denied anything or that I was at a disadvantage because my mom and my grandparents really did love me and took care of me, but some kids aren't as fortunate.

How does your foundation help kids who come from single-parent families?

We believe strongly in getting kids into a camp so they can be around the right people. There, a kid can evaluate his abilities and improve them, but most importantly he can have a change of heart and attitude. He can find out about leadership, character, and integrity, and he can go back to his high school and have an impact on teammates and peers. A lot of times we've seen evidence of a kid changing the heart and soul of a team. We hope to send a thousand kids to camp this year.

What's your favorite part about being a coach?

No other profession has more highs and lows. The satisfaction of seeing a kid or a team who had to struggle some to reach a level of success makes it worth it. My favorite team was a team that lost its first three games. I had no idea the direction this team was going to go. Sure enough, we ended up winning eight of our last nine games, and we ended 8-4. The way that team battled back was impressive. We had some great leadership. Seeing kids overcome adversity and disappointment was great.

What's the hardest part?

The toughest part is when you lose players like I did. My quarterback from 1986–1989 was Dee Dowis (who finished sixth in Heisman voting in 1989 and set the career rushing record for a quarterback). He tragically passed away recently, and I gave a eulogy at his funeral. I have given eulogies at the funerals of Coach Bost, Bell, and Brakefield. That's always tough, but it's one of the greatest honors of my life to have been asked to speak at their funerals.

Why does football matter?

Football is the ultimate team game. That's what we built our foundation on, a brotherhood. I found out when I was growing up in a little old country town that brothers are hard to beat. If one brother ever got in a fight, his other brother would jump in there and defend him. If you ever got in a fight with one brother, you'd be fighting the other brother soon enough. We always beat teams based on our brotherhood. That perpetuated itself at the Academy.

I always did something special for each senior class. My wife and I would have them come over, and we'd have a big barbecue and laugh and cut up with each other. Then we'd go down to the basement, and I'd give them pictures and write-ups from their time on the team for them to keep for their personal scrapbooks. And I always gave them a Bible that had the insignia of the helmet. I always told them that they'd had it pretty good, but there would be tough times in life and they needed something to rely on. I said they could always find answers in the Bible. I then told them that they needed to give back. So much had been given to them – their education didn't cost them anything. They were about to give back to this nation through their service, and I emphasized giving back no matter where they went in life.

The thing that's meant the most to me is the coaching tree. We have so many coaches today that are NFL assistants, college assistants, and Head Coaches, and high school coaches. I hope they gained that respect and enthusiasm for the game from our coaching staff.

HOW TO PICK THE RIGHT SYSTEM

The triple option really changed the game for Air Force Academy football. How was the decision made to try this unorthodox style of offense? During your time there, did you ever think about changing it?

I give Ken a lot of credit. In order for the Academy to be successful, we had to do something different. The idea of doing something different because of personnel was the idea. When I was Head Coach, I thought about changing the system sometimes, but then I thought the players would have revolted if that happened because they believed so strongly in what we were doing.

Our coaches did a great job implementing the system. And of course, today, since most teams don't run it, it's very difficult to defend against – especially if you just have one week to prepare for it.

How did you guys go about implementing the system, and how did you sell kids on it when you were recruiting?

You've got to believe in what you're doing as a coach and approach it with a very, very positive attitude. Then your kids will get on board. And all of a sudden, because of our success, we were able to develop a pipeline of high schools around the country that ran similar-style offenses.

Did it make it easier to recruit once you had a reputation for running this offense?

I think it did. Once you have a couple winning seasons at any school, people start to notice. We were so blessed to be able to attract the coaches we did. The Head Coach so often gets more credit than he deserves, but we were able to sell the whole idea of the Academy to people. You can achieve more at the Academy than you can at almost any other school in the country. You can have a chance to serve your nation, and if you decide to continue in the military, you can, or if you want to serve and then get out, you'll have great opportunities in the corporate world. We always sold the positive elements of our school instead of the negative parts of other schools.

Fisher DeBerry Career Stats

Career Record – 169-109-1

Conference Titles – 3

Consensus All-Americans – 3

Commander-in-Chief's Trophies – 14

AFCA, Bobby Dodd, Walter Camp, Paul "Bear" Bryant Coach of the Year – 1985

State Farm Coach of Distinction – 2001

College Football Hall of Fame – 2011

CHAPTER 5

Phillip Fulmer

HOW TO BOUNCE BACK FROM
DISAPPOINTMENT

"You have to control everything you can, and you manage the things you don't have control of. It's all about hustling for the ball. The attitude, the effort, and the execution you demand, along with managing the highs and lows a team experiences, give you your best chance to win a championship."

In 1997, the Tennessee Volunteers were quarter-backed by Peyton Manning and had 18 future NFL players on the roster, yet that team did not win the national championship.

An early loss to Florida and a season-ending loss to Nebraska prevented them from claiming the title. Manning graduated and went on to become the top pick in the NFL draft; also gone were star receiver Marcus Nash, linebacker Leonard Little, and others.

The 1998 Volunteers probably would have been forgiven for struggling a little bit. Instead, led by quarter-back Tee Martin and a solid defense, the Vols reeled off 13 straight wins en route to the very first BCS national title.

It would be Coach Phillip Fulmer's greatest coaching triumph, capping off a four-year run of 45-5. Fulmer's 17 years as Tennessee's Head Coach were preceded by 13 years as a Vols assistant and a four-year career as a guard for Tennessee. Coaching stints at Wichita State and Vanderbilt were the only years Fulmer hadn't spent coaching or playing in Knoxville.

Photo courtesy Tennessee Athletics.

Fulmer has the second-most wins in Tennessee history behind the legendary Robert Neyland, who spent 21 years as the Head Coach of the Vols.

Fulmer retired in 2008 and currently serves as a special advisor to the president at Tennessee. He was inducted into the College Football Hall of Fame in 2012.

What made you want to go into coaching?

I had such a wonderful upbringing with my parents in the little town of Winchester, Tennessee. It has about 10,000 folks. I tell people that to me it was about like Mayberry from *The Andy Griffith Show*. My Little League coaches were a huge influence on me. I had a great home life, and these guys were positive and encouraging and good mentors. Some are still friends today. I was very blessed to be around people very early in coaching that touched my life and made a difference. It was the same way in high school. College was a little different because it was a big business. But it was still a good experience.

When it came time to think about what I wanted to do, like everybody, I thought I'd be playing pro football or baseball somewhere. When I realized I needed to find something I was passionate about that wasn't playing a sport, I decided that I wanted to coach. I wasn't sure at what level, but I got an early start at Tennessee when Coach Bill Battle asked me to help out. I was thinking of going to law school, and I was taking some classes that I needed, but I ended up spending a lot more time in the film room than I did in the law library. I was very fortunate to get a start at 23 at Wichita State, which is really young. I actually coached two guys that were older than me.

Coaches Who Influenced Me

Childhood: Wayne Nuckolls, Ray Street, Jimmy Jacobs, Tippy Tipps

High school: Walter Bolden, Jackie Reavis, Jim Painter, Robert Osteen, Ralph Atkins, Joe Luhan

College: Doug Dickey (CFB Hall of Fame 2003), Bill Battle

What is something you remember from these coaches?

My high school coach actually dismissed every senior on the team for disciplinary reasons, and the youngsters that were left didn't win a game as sophomores. But we went on to become one of the best teams in the state. Nine of those guys went on to play in the Southeastern Conference, and 27 got football scholarships. That group of kids changed the culture of our high school team, our school, and our community.

What was your favorite part of coaching?

I think all the coaches will tell you that it's the players and the relationships you have with kids. Even being out now, I hear from them every day in some way or another. I loved the game and practice and recruiting. There wasn't much I disliked. Also, to go to LSU or Florida or Georgia and win was stimulating to say the least.

What was the hardest part?

The time away from your family. Some people may have done a better job than others. I didn't do as good a job as I should have. It was almost like you were more afraid of losing than you were craving the thrill of victory, so that led to staying too long at the office sometimes.

What is your No. 1 piece of advice that you would give a young coach?

To be successful at anything, you've got to have a passion for it. You've got to be committed to it every day and grow as a young guy. I'd say that you need to be sure to communicate. We had a special relationship with a lot of my coaches. We could absolutely close the door and be on the same page when we came out. It's really difficult to be successful if you aren't on the same page. A lot of guys want to get into it because they think it's glamorous, but you have to have a passion for the kids.

Why does football matter?

Because of the discipline, camaraderie, and teamwork that it teaches. I use those every day in life. People often think that it just comes easy, but football teaches you that you have to earn everything that you get. It teaches those life lessons that are not easily found at an early age.

HOW TO BOUNCE BACK FROM

DISAPPOINTMENT

The 1997 season ended in disappointment, despite having a great team. Then, you lost Peyton Manning, Leonard Little, Marcus Nash, and others to the NFL Draft. Yet the 1998 season ended with a 13-0 record

and your team holding the very first BCS National Championship Trophy. How did you rally your team after the disappointment of 1997?

Those teams were obviously all really special – 1995, 1997, 1999, and 2001. If there was a College Football Playoff like there is now, I think we would have been in it those years, as would have Florida. The two of us were among the best teams in the country during those years.

It was a mind-set that we had at that particular stretch there. It was a culture that was really, really special. We actually lost 12 guys to the NFL. Losing a guy like Peyton was especially tough, but we had all the pieces, especially on defense.

To win a national championship, you have to be really talented, well coached, and a little lucky too. That year we had some breaks go our way, whereas in 1995 and 1997, we didn't get the breaks. It comes down to making a play or two in a big ball game, or the ball bouncing your way one time, that makes a difference.

The kids were passionate and determined. They rallied around QB Tee Martin. It was almost like they weren't going to let him fail. He really commanded them and did a great job in the off-season. If they had independent throwing practice, they would all be there.

You mentioned the mind-set that your team had. How did you create a culture that fostered that mind-set?

I think it was the consistency of the coaches. The family atmosphere that we had. We recruited really, really well during that time. It was all of those factors. The biggest thing was those kids. We had a tough loss in '97 at Florida and then at the end of the year to Nebraska in the Orange Bowl. They came into the off-season more determined than ever. Rather than being disappointed, they were determined to go get it done. We hardly had any issues that would distract us in any way. We focused our football team well.

Did you do anything special that year to help your team focus?

My wife and I hike in the mountains sometimes, and a friend sent me a really nice carved walking stick. I happened to be going to practice when it was delivered, so I took it to practice with me. I asked the guys if they liked my walking stick, and they said I looked like Moses. That night I was thinking about how Moses led his team to the Promised Land.

So the next day I called the team together and put them in a big circle instead of the rows they usually sat in. That kind of baffled them. I said, "You guys were having some fun with me yesterday, calling me Moses. But Moses led his people to the Promised Land. I'm telling you guys right now, if you listen, I'm going to lead you to the National Championship Promised Land. This stick that you guys were making fun of yesterday is going to be the center of our energy. It's going to be our Synergy Stick."

I thought it was so corny, but the guys totally bought it. I don't know what part that played, but I think it really refocused our team. We were undefeated at the time, but we hadn't played great yet. From that point on, that stick was the first thing on the plane, first thing off the bus, first thing on the sideline. I told them not to tell anyone – not their parents, their girlfriends, and most of all, not the media. It was just between us.

Focus is hard to get and keep, but that darn Synergy Stick focused our football team.

Did the stick help remind them to focus on each day instead of eyeing the big games like Florida, Georgia, or Arkansas?

I think the kids were really focused, and they knew they had something special. We had the schedule to get to the national championship that year. It was something they weren't going to be denied. They went to practice every day to get better. My staff did a great job. We took it one game at a time. We had to fight our rears off – we weren't quite as talented as we had been the last couple of years. The thing is, you don't have to be the best team in the country. You just have to be the best team on the field where you're playing each Saturday.

You've mentioned a few times about the breaks your team got in 1998 that you didn't get in other years. How do those affect your season, and how can you prepare your team to react to things outside their control?

Almost every year, when you look at the national championship, there's some place in there where the team is fortunate. There's always a play here or there that you go back and make to win, or you don't make to lose. Our 1997 team may have been a play or two away from beating Florida. You don't know when those plays are going to come, but you know they're going to come and you have to make the play.

You have to control everything you can, and you manage the things you don't have control of. It's all about hustling for the ball. We had a defensive tackle named Billy Ratliff that recovered a fumble 15 yards down the field against Florida – because he was hustling. That's how you win championships. It was late in the game, too. You might think everybody hustles, but that's not the case. The attitude, the effort, and the execution you demand, along with managing the highs and lows a team experiences, give you your best chance to win a championship.

Phillip Fulmer Career Stats

Career Record – 152-52

National Championships – 1

Conference Titles – 2

Consensus All-Americans – 8

William V. Campbell Trophy Winners – 2
(Peyton Manning 1997; Michael Munoz 2004)

AFCA, Eddie Robinson, George Munger, Home Depot, Sporting News Coach of the Year – 1998

College Football Hall of Fame – 2012

Handling Players

CHAPTER 6

R.C. Slocum

HOW TO RUN A CLEAN PROGRAM AND TREAT PLAYERS THE RIGHT WAY

"You've got to do things like you believe they should be done. When it's all said and done and the smoke clears, you want to look at yourself and say, 'I did what I thought should be done, and I did it like I thought it should be done.'"

In the over 120-year history of Texas A&M football, some legendary coaches have spent time in College Station with the Aggies.

Dana X. Bible, Matty Bell, Gene Stallings, Homer Norton, and Paul "Bear" Bryant are all College Football Hall of Famers, but it would be difficult to argue that any surpass R.C. Slocum in terms of success in Aggieland.

Slocum owns more Aggie wins than any of those other coaches (123). In Slocum's 14 years patrolling the sidelines, he lost only 12 games, including only four losses at Kyle Field in the 1990s. The Aggies won four conference championships and were the dominant team as the Southwest Conference ended and transitioned into the Big 12.

When Slocum took over the A&M football team, however, the team was under a two-year probation imposed by the NCAA due to numerous violations. A widely respected coach on and off the field, Slocum set out to run a clean, but winning program. His tenure was marked by reforms that saw the Aggies emerge from the shadows of the '80s and produce superstar defensive players and leaders like 2017 College Football Hall of Famer Dat Nguyen.

Photo courtesy of Glen Johnson/Texas A&M Athletics.

Slocum, who grew up in Orange, Texas, played football at McNeese State in Lake Charles, Louisiana. Texas A&M was the only head-coaching job he ever held. Through a variety of roles at Texas A&M, he remains active in the Aggie community and was inducted into the College Football Hall of Fame in 2012.

.

What made you want to go into coaching?

The answer to that is really easy. I grew up in southeast Texas, in Orange. No one in my family had been to college. They were hardworking people, but we actually spent time in the projects when I was young. I shined shoes, had a paper route, and did whatever I could to help make ends meet.

In seventh-grade PE class, one of the coaches called me over and said, "How come you're not out for football?" I didn't really know why. My family wasn't into football; my dad never played and didn't know anything about it, so I just never had played. And that coach said, "Well, I think you could play."

So I went home to ask my parents. To be honest, they weren't all that excited about it. They weren't negative about it, but they just didn't know anything about the sport. I went out for football and made the team. I ended up having a great career through high school. I was on a good team, and with the help of my coaches – who taught me and molded me and polished me – I was able to get a scholarship to college. I was the first in my family to go to college.

So when it came time to pick a profession, I knew that coaching was what I wanted to do. It was a direct reflection of the influence that my coaches had on me and the strong respect I had for them and what the game of football meant to me. I thought, "If I could play that role in some other young men's lives, that would be a heck of a way to earn a living."

That's all I ever wanted to do, and that's all I've ever done.

Who are the coaches that stood out? What did they teach you about coaching?

All the way through, I could say I never had a bad coach. I always had guys that cared about me. They worked me very hard, but there never was a coach that I didn't think really cared about me. I thought every coach was like that. When I got into coaching, I realized that not all coaches are that way, but I thought that was the main role of a coach.

Obviously you've got to teach football. The game of football is a fun game; it means a whole lot to me – I love it. I have to say, though, that I've always felt that the most important thing that a coach did was impact those lives that were entrusted to him. For junior and senior high guys, you've got those guys in there that look up to you. You've got a chance, by example, to mold and direct them. And when you're a college coach, you spend a lot of time with those guys at a very formative time in their lives.

A coach can have a great influence on a young man. That's the ultimate measure of a coach. If you look five or ten years down the road at the young men he had under his leadership and see what kind of people they are, that's the measure of a coach. The wins and losses over time run together, but that's not the single-best measure of the performance of a coach. I've known guys over the years that did win some games, but the way they won the games? I would have given them a losing score in the end.

I'm a Christian, and I always operated with the idea that there is a Big Head Coach somewhere that wasn't worried about whether I went for it on fourth down. He would say, "I gave you 100+ young men to lead and influence. Let's talk about how you used your position."

It was very important, having those guys that were looking for leadership. I would go into a home, recruit a young man, and have a mother turn him over to me and entrust me with him and his development. I saw that as a very important role that I was playing.

What is the hardest part of being a coach?

It's meaningful. It's not easy. If you're a parent raising kids, it's not easy. If you're a coach managing 100+ guys from different backgrounds, it's not easy – especially at that age. They're away from home for the first time, and they're going through that phase where they aren't settled on who they are or what they are or where they're going. To be a person that's involved in that with a young man isn't easy.

It's important to have the courage as a coach to say, "You might have your buddies, but I am not your buddy. I'm your coach, I'm your mentor, and in some cases, your father figure. It's not in your or my best interest to always say yes to you. My job is to be honest with you and give you the hard truths and lessons that, in the long run, will help you be a better man. I'm going to be totally honest with you, and I'm not going to sugarcoat it – because I want to try to help you be better."

I'm very proud to be in the College Football Hall of Fame, but the most meaningful thing is the players that I see and hear from on a daily basis. To be able to see the kinds of people they are now is the most meaningful thing in my life now, apart from my immediate family.

What is your No. 1 piece of advice that you would give to a young coach?

I read a book by a guy named Joe Ehrmann called *In-SideOut Coaching*. He said that every coach should ask himself three questions:

"Why do I coach?" – I coach because of the men that influenced and changed my life.

"How do I coach?" – Am I a guy that grabs kids and shakes them and curses them?

"What would it be like to be coached by me?" – What kind of recollection would a guy have five or ten years down the road about me?

If you can answer all of those questions, then you'll be fine. Do you coach because you want to be a positive influence on kids? Or do you coach because you want recognition and the attention? Or do you want to make a lot of money?

I'm concerned that some coaches are in it just to make a lot of money. I can assure you that none of the guys my age that coached did it for the money – that wasn't even a consideration. We did it because it was a chance for us to give back and do something that had been very meaningful in our lives.

Why does football matter?

Football matters because it's one of the few activities left that mirrors life. The lessons that can be learned from the game of football directly reflect the lessons of life.

Things won't always go your way. You're going to get beat for a touchdown; you're going to throw an interception; the guy on the other side of the ball will beat you. One of the real keys to success is overcoming that disappointment. To be able to deal with that disappointment and not let it get you down – to use that as motivation – that's an important lesson in life.

Inversely, things will go really well. When you have a great game, the lesson to learn is not to get too carried away with your successes. There were other people involved in whatever you did. Football is a team sport, like life. There are very few things that you did solely on your own.

I've got a picture in my office that I'm looking at right now. It's a picture of the 1998 Big 12 Championship Trophy. It was taken in the locker room after the game. I had everybody gather around, and I had as many guys as possible hold the trophy up. Then I told the team to look. We had black hands, white hands, mixed-race hands, Vietnamese hands, and Tongan hands. This was a great example of the lesson of what happens when you can all work together.

Another great lesson is learning how to be successful as a backup player. Instead of pouting and feeling sorry for yourself and thinking the coach is unfair, there's a lesson to be learned from being the best backup so that when the opportunity comes, you're ready to play. I think a lot of young kids come out of college and go to work and if they aren't president of the company in the first year, then they're looking for another job. They should be supportive of the guy in front of them and work hard and then, when their turn comes, they can be ready for it.

Football teaches people to work together, and Lord knows, we need it in our country right now. On every team and in every season, you're going to have problems. But you work those problems out if you're going to have a good team. You don't think in terms of white, black, Vietnamese, or Hispanic players. You just think in terms of "our team" and "our guys." Football is one of the only places right now where that can happen.

And it's a tough sport. If you look at the history of our nation, we've been successful because we've been strong, tough people. If you look at World War II, our nation's existence depended on having strong, resilient people. Football is one of the few places that teaches toughness. Toughness is important. It's important to be able to do something that's hard. When it's hot, you don't go sit inside. You work through it. You learn how to work through difficulty. You learn how to work through a tough opponent. You learn how not to give into the soft side of yourself.

If you asked a bunch of young people, "Other than your parents, who is the most significant person in your life?" so many of them would say their coach. The word "coach" is a significant title and a great honor, but it also bears significant responsibility.

HOW TO RUN A CLEAN PROGRAM AND TREAT

PLAYERS THE RIGHT WAY

What's something a coach can do on Day One to make sure they win the right way?

I think the Head Coach sets the tone and the culture. When you hire people, it's important to make it very clear what you're all about and what you intend to do with the program. Ultimately the Head Coach is responsible for what happens with the program anyway. I think it's really important that you set the groundwork.

I told my guys that they couldn't pick and choose the rules they go by. There were some rules that didn't make sense. There's always a system to get rules changed if needed. But so long as it's a rule, you can't choose whether you follow it or not.

I told my guys that I didn't want to be even close to the line. I didn't want to tiptoe to the line and see how close we could get. Sooner or later, you'll end up over the line. I wanted a clear separation between what was allowed by the rules and what we were doing. I wanted the players to understand that too.

I'm not going to go into a home to recruit a parent's most prized possession and then teach him how to cheat. Over the years, I've had players tell me that they have kids now and they finally understand why I was the way that I was. That's really meaningful – to know that I made a meaningful impression on them.

We made it a point to be clear with the players and the coaches that this is how we're doing things. What happens is you have players leave and assistant coaches take other jobs, and pretty soon what you are becomes what you are. I used to tell the players that we all get to make our reputations. As guys leave, then what you are inside your program gets spread around, and your reputation spreads throughout the game. It was always important to me that people had a positive impression of us and our program. We wanted to be known as an honorable program.

That's one of the other lasting things – that reputation. As I go around the state and the country, I get to have a relationship of mutual respect with coaches that I coached against. I used to go on a golf trip once a year with former Texas Coach Mack Brown and former Texas Tech Coach Spike Dykes. We all competed against each other and tried hard to win games, but there's a mutual admiration and respect about how we did those things. I would much rather have that than to have won a few more games and have those guys not want to be around me because I was crooked.

Do you feel like you ever missed out on a recruit because you stuck so strongly to the rules?

It balances out. We probably gained some guys because we had that reputation. I did this in every home. I said, "Number one, I wouldn't be here if I didn't think your son is a good person. I will pledge to you that I will do everything that I can as a Head Coach to keep your son pointed in the direction that I think he is headed in right now. If I didn't think he was a good person, I wouldn't even be here. And I will try to recruit people like your son to keep him on a good path.

"The second thing I want him to understand is the importance of getting an education. I'm not saying he's got to jump up and down and love school. He needs to understand how important his education is, and that way he will understand why it's important to go to class and keep up with his schoolwork.

"And the third thing is, I want him to be burning up with a desire to be a great football player. And that's the order and I pledge to keep it in that order."

So one year, when we were getting ready to play Oklahoma, I had players come to me and say that they had a departmental study session that was at five o'clock. That was when we had practice. So I thought back in my mind to the pledge I had made to those players, and now I'm called on the carpet to see if I really meant what I told those parents. I told the guys to come to practice and, when the time came, to go shower up and go to their study session. Those are things that the fans and alumni never know about, but I felt it was important, based on what I told the parents and those young men. I would have lost credibility if I had valued the game over academics.

Just being a man of your word may be an old-fashioned idea, but I still believe in it. If you tell somebody something, then it should mean something. I think it's vitally important. You've got young men that are very impressionable. Teaching football is fun, but it won't get them through life.

I met a guy on a plane once that was a speech and communications professor here named Dr. Rick Rigsby. He was also kind of a lay minister. I was sitting on a plane with him, and I was so impressed with the guy. We got together later, and the more I talked to him, the more impressed I was and I said, "I got a job for you. We can teach these kids the Cover 2, but we need to bring someone in to help teach life skills to these guys."

We created a part-time position where he was a counselor-chaplain-motivator, a "character coach." All our freshmen would take a class once a week on character issues, like being honest. What does it mean to be honest, or to be respectful? We had sessions where we booked time every week with those kids to just hammer away at those issues.

I had a team devotional every Saturday before every game I ever coached. It was optional, but we had over 90 percent attendance at those. We just wanted to say that the game was important, but there are things that are way more important. And hey, we won enough games that I made it into the College Football Hall of Fame, so we won some games. But I think putting first things first actually helped us win those games.

Is it harder in today's world to do things the right way?

I don't know the answer to that. I felt this way when I coached, and I feel this way now: You first have to be true to yourself. You've got to do things like you believe they should be done. When it's all said and done and the smoke clears, you want to look at yourself and say, "I did what I thought should be done, and I did it like I thought it should be done."

You'd hate to look back and realize that you didn't do it like you wanted to, even if you had a little success. I told the coaches I had that, if we do the right things and we get enough of the right people in here, then we'll win games and we'll have something to be proud of.

One time, I had a coach that didn't really fit that mold in terms of his language and the way he talked to kids. Early on, in the first spring, I could not believe the way I saw him talking to these kids. I sat down with him and said, "We went out and recruited these parents' most prized possessions. I have two sons, and I don't want anyone cursing them. So I'm not going to curse some other mother's son." I told parents that they were always welcome to come to practice, and I didn't want to have to run down to this coach to warn him that some parent was there so he would clean up his language.

Over the course of the year, I figured out that when I was around, he would clean it up, but if I was on the other end of the field, he would change it. So at the end of the year, I said, "You're apparently set in your ways, and you don't want to change or are unable to change. On the other hand, I'm set in my ways, too, and I'm too old to change. There are some people that would probably appreciate the way you coach and handle young people, but that's not how we do it here. So you need to go find you another job."

I had a picture of how we treated people, and I wasn't going to change that. I made a stand. It's unbelievable how some of these guys talk to young people, but they have to live with that.

We worked hard, but I never cursed these kids, and I never allowed my coaches to do it.

Do the money, pressure, and scrutiny make it difficult?

I don't think the coach gets the same amount of support these days. Nowadays, parents are so overbearing with high school coaches. A coach might be doing a good job mentoring the kids, but a parent is too worried that the coach might be costing the kid a scholarship.

This might not be popular, but we have some parents that don't have enough courage to be a parent. They want to be their kid's buddies and not their parents. Being a parent doesn't mean always saying yes. They can have buddies in school that they run around with. As a parent, you've got a tremendous responsibility to try to mold their character to get them ready to go out into this world to be successful and have productive lives.

If I were coaching today, I'd be coaching exactly the same. I would say, "I care about you – you're my guy. I'm going to do everything I can to get you on a track that will help you be successful."

I used to tell them, "When we get off the bus to go to the hotel, it's important to carry yourselves in a good manner because in just a few short years, I'll be calling some of the people standing here, and I'll be telling them why you're a good candidate to work for them."

I wanted my players to conduct themselves in a positive way so that they could stand out as somebody special.

R.C. Slocum Career Stats

Career Record – 123-47-2

Conference Titles – 4

Consensus All-Americans – 7

College Football Hall of Fame – 2012

Amos Alonzo Stagg Award – 2014

CHAPTER 7

Terry Donahue

HOW TO KEEP PLAYERS FROM DISTRACTIONS

"It was truly a balancing act. We didn't want somebody to come to LA for the nightlife. We wanted somebody who wanted to come to UCLA, get an education, play on our team and play in the Rose Bowl. But we didn't try to downplay the fact that we were in LA. We tried to attract athletes that were interested in that kind of environment."

Convincing an 18-year-old to move to Los Angeles for college is a seemingly easy task. The beach, the mountains, the desert, the fun, the girls, the nightlife, and – oh yeah, the great education and football.

Where things get tricky is getting said 18-year-old to concentrate on football and school when surrounded by all of those distractions. Terry Donahue knows all about keeping kids concentrated on football and the classroom.

During his 20-year tenure at the helm of the UCLA Bruins football team, Donahue led the team to three Rose Bowl victories and five conference titles.

Coaching in the same city as the vaunted USC program, Donahue was constantly recruiting against the Trojans. He had a winning career record against USC – quite a feat, considering the overall head-to-head record puts the Trojans up by double-digits over the Bruins.

Photo courtesy of Don Liebig/UCLA Athletics.

Donahue played defensive end at UCLA and began his coaching career under Pepper Rodgers at Kansas before moving back to Los Angeles when Rodgers took the UCLA job in 1971. After Rodgers left UCLA to return to Georgia Tech, his alma mater, Donahue was promoted. He would keep the job for two decades of unprecedented success in Westwood. Donahue's 151 career wins are more than double that of UCLA's second-winningest coach, William H. Spaulding.

After stepping down as UCLA's Head Coach in 1995, Donahue became the general manager of the San Francisco 49ers for four seasons. These days, he presents the California Showcase, which is a one-day event for high school players to showcase their skills to Division II, III, and NAIA schools. He was inducted into the College Football Hall of Fame in 2000.

What made you want to go into coaching?

I always loved football. I played in high school and college, and I wanted to play professionally but I wasn't big enough or skilled enough for that. So when I got out of college, I wanted to stay connected to football, and it seemed like coaching would be a natural progression.

I just decided to try and become a coach. I had great respect and appreciation for my coaches, particularly Tommy Prothro and his staff at UCLA. I admired those guys and thought that I'd like to become a coach.

I had to go into the service, and when I came out, I got the opportunity of a lifetime when Pepper Rodgers hired me at the University of Kansas. He was a coach at UCLA when I played there, and he gave me the opportunity to go to Kansas as a volunteer coach.

I worked for nothing, but I got the chance to learn how to coach. That was the break I needed to get started. If it hadn't been for people like Pepper Rodgers, John Cooper, Tommy Prothro, and my high school coaches, my life would have been very, very different.

What was your favorite part about coaching?

At the time, it was just being a coach, being involved in football, being in charge of a group of guys, and competing and performing. Later, as you mature as a coach and you gain insight into what it's truly about, you realize that the teaching aspect of coaching and the relationship you have with the players comes to the forefront – particularly as you get older and you see the players you coached and recruited, and you see the kinds of guys they become, the families they have, the careers they develop, and all the different things that they do. That relationship, far and away, becomes the most important part of coaching.

What was the hardest part?

The hardest part is the fact that there's such pressure to win. That's far and away the most difficult thing. It causes you to put too much pressure on your players and your coaches. It causes people to violate their ethical standards. Sometimes it causes you to become embittered with certain situations. The constant criticism that a coach is under when he's not winning can be the most difficult part of it.

You read some of these critical articles, and you would think the coach is intentionally not trying to win. Some of these fans are so critical, but I guarantee you, if you examined their lives and careers and failures, they're in just as bad of a situation as the coach who's having a bad season.

Particularly now in our society, there's so much demand for instant gratification and performance that coaches are under a lot of scrutiny. If it wasn't like that, then coaches would do a better job long-term and be able to really concentrate and emphasize the more important aspects of coaching as opposed to just winning. We all want to win and you have to win enough, but at the same time, it can lead to a lot of bad things, too.

What's the No. 1 piece of advice that you would give a young coach?

I would say, number one, establish your core values and do some introspection in terms of what you're trying to accomplish as a coach. Number two, there are so many great resources for young coaches. There are so many books written by outstanding coaches who had great careers. Those books contain a lot of valuable knowledge. When you become a coach, there's not necessarily a manual. You're usually an assistant and then you become a coach, and it's not necessarily because you're the best coach. There used to be no road map or resources that could teach you how to do it, but now you could pick up a great coach's book and learn from it. For example, you could read Grant Teaff's book *Football Coaching Strategies* and learn from his career, the different things he learned, the challenges he faced, and the decisions he made along the road. It would give you such a great resource to put together with your own core values. It would help you navigate the difficulties of coaching.

Why does football matter?

Football matters for a lot of reasons. It teaches you about a team concept. For most of us as we progress through our lives, we're going to be involved in a team concept, either as a leader or a member of a team. Football, more than anything I've ever seen, teaches you about that. It teaches that you, as an individual, are not automatically first and foremost. The greater good takes precedence over your particular interests and desires. I think football is a great teaching tool.

Like any team sport, it teaches you about winning and losing. It teaches you about bonding and working with individuals and being tolerant of others' differences. There are so many diverse personalities and agendas. Many of the things we face in our difficult society today disappear in a football team's atmosphere. It just doesn't exist in the locker room. It shows you how great things could be if everybody could interact and react with each other as most football teams do – especially when they're having difficult seasons. Football imparts the values of competition, winning, losing, and sacrifice. It imparts the values of all the different things that a lot of us believe in. There's no greater environment to learn all of those lessons than football.

HOW TO KEEP PLAYERS FROM DISTRACTIONS

Los Angeles is a city with unlimited opportunities and fun, but it could also distract a young man from his duties as a student and a football player. How did you make sure to keep your players focused on the field and in the classroom?

I wish we had a magic formula that would have helped us. As you mentioned, Los Angeles has many, many distractions. That can be a blessing and a curse. It's a blessing in the sense that sometimes it's nice that the grocery clerk doesn't get on to you for not winning that week. That can happen in a smaller environment where everything and everybody is focused on the game. The flip side of that is true, too. You can win a big game and the grocery clerk doesn't know about that either.

In a big environment like Los Angeles, you probably spend more time trying to counsel your players about the distractions and dangers that are out there, and you have a harder time trying to make sure that you're on top of your players in terms of them doing the right things and not getting into difficult situations. It's very, very challenging and extremely hard to do. Los Angeles can present so many different things to a young kid. You have to continually talk about it and stress it and make it something that everybody is aware of.

Those same things are what attract young people. They want a big city with a lot of opportunities and diversity. It just depends on what a kid is looking for and what he wants out of his college experience. We spend a lot of time trying to explain to our players what they have to be careful of.

When you recruited players, did you recruit kids that you thought could handle the big city?

That kind of sorted itself out. For example, if we recruited somebody from rural Tennessee, they would for sure take a trip to see Los Angeles and UCLA. They might have a wonderful weekend, but they'd eventually figure out that they didn't fit out here. They might have enjoyed their time, but they knew that they'd be happier in a more rural setting. On the other hand, some kids from those types of backgrounds come out here and think that a big city is exactly what they're looking for.

Frankly, it was a vetting process where kids would vet themselves. They'd decide if the environment was what they were looking for. We never said whether a guy would fit in or not because guys know that themselves, even though there were clearly some kids that we could tell would have a very difficult time because the city can be so overwhelming.

On the topic of recruiting, obviously selling Los Angeles as a destination is a big part of attracting someone to UCLA. Did you have to balance how much you sold the city while still trying to make sure kids were coming for the right reasons?

It was truly a balancing act. We didn't want somebody to come to LA for the nightlife. We wanted somebody who wanted to come to UCLA, get an education, play on our team, and play in the Rose Bowl. But we'd certainly sell the beach and the mountains and the desert and the fact that, when you weren't involved in football, you were going to have a lot to do. We sold that very hard and tried to play to our strength. We didn't try to downplay the fact that we were in LA. We took advantage of the Lakers, Dodgers, Angels, or whoever was playing well at the time. We tried to attract athletes that were interested in that kind of environment.

You talked about Los Angeles being a gift and a curse when it comes to distractions and pressure. As your teams began to have success, did the pressure increase and make it more difficult to focus on the field?

There was always lots of pressure because the media was constantly putting us under the spotlight. There was

a great deal of scrutiny and critiquing, analyzing and se-
cond-guessing. This is a very fragmented city. It isn't
like Columbus, Ohio, where 99 percent of the people are
rooting for the home team. You have both UCLA and
USC in Los Angeles, so automatically half the people
are rooting against you. That's a very challenging environment.

Even though that grocery clerk might not know who
you are, the *Los Angeles Times* and the other newspapers
had a job to do. You were always under the gun to perform in LA. There was a very high expectation level for
all the teams because of the influence of pro sports. The
expectation level from teams like the Lakers and Dodgers was carried on to USC and UCLA.

**Coaching in a city where half the city is against
you is rare in college. Did you counsel your players on
how to handle the intensity of the rivalry? Did that
make it more difficult to coach and recruit when your
rival was so close?**

We never made much of a point of that. People figured it out. It was like a range war out here. You were
either a UCLA or a USC guy. That's what made it so
unique and different from any other rivalry in the country. There are so many great rivalries in the country, but
the most unique rivalry of all of them is UCLA and USC
because it's the only major rivalry that shares the same
city. That gives it a unique flavor and a unique level of
intensity. It's one of the things that makes it so difficult

to coach in a city like Los Angeles. You have a really storied football program 12 miles from your school. If they're winning and you aren't, then you have a real problem, and vice versa. It really intensifies your situation.

We had players that lived with players on USC's team, so the week of the game, you never dared send home a scouting report. A lot of them grew up together playing on the same high school team. It was a very unique situation. Guys would share summer jobs or go to the same parties. It's a reason why the game becomes so intense.

Terry Donahue Career Stats

Career Record – 151-74-8

Conference Titles – 5

Consensus All-Americans – 12

College Football Hall of Fame – 2000

CHAPTER 8

Vince Dooley

HOW TO HANDLE SUPERSTARS

"Superstars don't all come in the same package. Some are much more challenging than others. Herschel just happened to be the easiest possible person to coach. If you had just one superstar and you had Herschel Walker, then you might be spoiled into thinking that you have all the answers on how to handle them. It's like children — some are much easier than others."

Vince Dooley's 25-year reign as the Head Coach of the Georgia Bulldogs was one of consistent excellence that peaked during the 1980–1984 seasons in which Dooley's Bulldogs had the best record in all of college football. The 1980 season was his lone national championship, with three of his six SEC conference titles being won between 1980 and 1983.

The key factor in the first three of those seasons was the dominance of running back Herschel Walker. The 1982 Heisman Trophy winner, Walker announced himself to the college football world in his first game as a freshman, rushing for two touchdowns, including his iconic first TD in which he ran over Tennessee safety Bill Bates on the way to the end zone.

Georgia, with its dominant defense led by longtime assistant coach Erskine "Erk" Russell and College Football Hall of Fame safety Scott Woerner, would ride Herschel Walker to the 1980 national championship. Walker was a bona-fide superstar.

Photo courtesy of UGA Athletic Association..

But Dooley proved that his team wasn't just about the superstar once Walker left early for the USFL after his junior year. The Bulldogs would finish the 1983 season by defeating No. 2 Texas in the Cotton Bowl. They were ranked No. 4 in the final AP Poll, behind Miami, Nebraska, and Auburn, who all had only one loss (Georgia had a loss and a tie).

Dooley played quarterback at Auburn (1950–53) and was an assistant under Shug Jordan for eight seasons (1956–1963). He served as the Georgia Athletics Director from 1979 to 2004, with Bulldog teams winning 20 national championships and 78 SEC championships during that time. More recently, he served as a consultant for Kennesaw State (in Georgia) as they started a football program, which began playing in 2014. He was inducted into the College Football Hall of Fame in 1994.

What made you want to go into coaching?

I really wasn't sure what I wanted to do after I graduated, but I had great respect for my high school coach. Outside my parents, he exerted more influence on me than anyone else . His positive influence was particularly important during the critically formative high school days. I always had a great appreciation for the impact high school coaches can have on people at a formative age. That was the case for me.

A lot of things didn't make sense to me as a young teenager trying to find my way – but sports did! It was through sports that the coach had a positive influence on me and got me going in the right direction. His influence on me was the main reason that I wanted to get into coaching and be in a position to do the same thing.

In college, I was a business major; then I had obligations to serve in the military, and I chose the Marine Corps. There was no need to make any immediate decision about my future. It was already laid out. That came later, after my obligation of two years of active duty was up.

I had four opportunities when it was time to make a decision about my future. One was to stay in the Marine Corps. I really enjoyed my experience, especially the discipline and the organization. I had an offer to go back to my hometown and work in the banking business. I also had an offer to coach at the high school in Mobile where I attended and played, and I had an offer to return to Auburn as an assistant coach. The most appealing of all those offers was the opportunity to go back to my college alma mater as an assistant coach. It was too much of an opportunity to pass up, and I wanted to see if I was totally committed to coaching. Once I started coaching, I knew I'd made the right decision.

Coaches Who Influenced Me

High School: Ray Dicharry

College: Ralph "Shug" Jordan (CFB Hall Class of 1982)

What confirmed to you that coaching should be your career? Did you get any experience under your belt before returning to Auburn?

In the Marine Corps I experienced team building, leadership, and discipline. Those values appeal to me as a Marine and as a coach, and I drew from my military experience throughout my career as a coach. The idea that you can influence people in a positive way was appealing as well.

I played football in the Marine Corps for a year and then coached another year. That was my first experience coaching – other than the fact that, as the quarterback and captain of my college team, I was considered a "coach on the field," as Coach Jordan often said.

What was the hardest part about being a coach?

The demands of balancing an all-consuming work schedule and raising a family was a daunting challenge. My kids and Barbara suffered a little bit in that respect. I was fortunate to marry a woman that had a real commitment to be a wife and a mother. Fortunately, our kids went to a high school where the coach was like a second father to them. If I was gone and Barbara needed a strong hand to handle a problem with the children, she could call on their high school coach, Billy Henderson, or his son-in-law, Coach Steve Brooks. They both are outstanding human beings. I was able to handle the biggest challenge of being a coach because of having people like them that helped us out.

What is the No. 1 piece of advice you give a young coach?

It is really important to be totally committed to it. It's a very satisfying profession, but very demanding, so addressing the family challenge is critical. It's important to always remind oneself of the influence (good or bad) that one can have on his players. It's very challenging because the expectations are so high. The other
challenge is to balance your life with a family, so a good soulmate is paramount. Once you've satisfied all those things, then you're off and running.

Why does football matter?

I think it provides a culture and a brand, particularly to an institution. We see that today with the incredible number of schools that are starting football programs, even though financially it's a challenge. I've been involved in consulting with Kennesaw State's new football program. It gives people that culture and pride in a color, a mascot, a fight song. Those rallying cries tend to bind people together for a lifetime, and that's an overall benefit for the institution. People want to be part of a team. They want to be part of something special.

Plus, young people like to compete. There's no other sport where teamwork is more important than in football. It involves so many different people working together for a common cause. All the lessons from football and sports in general – such as discipline, sacrifice, and hard work – have lifelong carry-over values. You'll see individuals today that refer back to their high school or college coach and the lessons they learned from their playing days. I think all of that has an incredible appeal to the individual and the institutions.

HOW TO HANDLE SUPERSTARS

Herschel Walker was undoubtedly a superstar. What made Herschel special? What kind of person

was he? Was he like any other superstar you coached?

Superstars don't all come in the same package. Some are much more challenging than others. Herschel just happened to be the easiest possible person to coach. If you had just one superstar and you had Herschel Walker, then you might be spoiled into thinking that you have all the answers on how to handle them. It's like children – some are much easier than others.

I've had challenges from superstars, and I've had Herschel, who was the easiest one to handle. He had a great ability to always say the right thing. He was all about the team. He was so self-disciplined, probably the most self-disciplined athlete that I've ever been around. Even today he's probably the best-conditioned 55-year-old man in the world. He has an incredible work ethic. The Good Lord blessed him early on with a great body and speed.

Why do you think Herschel worked so hard?

Even though he was from a very small school, he was motivated to improve. One reason is that he had a sister, Veronica, who was older than him and faster than him at an early age. That challenged him. They didn't even have a weight program at his high school, and he wanted to get stronger. His high school coach told him to do push-ups. That's all you have to do is tell Herschel to do something. He did push-ups during every commercial when he was watching television. He may still be doing so today. He would do front push-ups, back push-ups, one-armed push-ups, push-ups with people on his back. He even wrote a book on push-ups. That's an example of how self-disciplined he was.

He was also a good student. He wanted to do well in whatever he did. He had an engaging way and a humility about him, and, of course, he was extremely competitive. He was always one of the first ones to show up for a team meeting, and he'd sit erect, almost at attention. He was such an example. His response to everything was that he wanted to please his coaches and his teammates. He was such a great role model.

So Herschel was the ideal. Did you ever have a superstar that was less than ideal? How did you handle them?

There was another superstar I had that was more a free spirit. He was ahead of his time as a free spirit, and he was much more challenging. It was a question of going the extra mile to help him but never crossing the line where it could hurt the mission of the team. Whenever I felt like it affected the team, I had to come down hard. I used that as a measure in the application of discipline. Superstars come in a variety of packages.

Some of the most challenging superstars I had were great players who were all about competing and winning. However, there weren't a lot of other responsibilities that were important to them. I would try to understand and work with them until I felt that they were doing things that affected team unity, and then I had to strongly address the situation.

How do you know when to discipline a player and when to work with them?

When you get the sense that the individual's actions are affecting the overall performance of the team, you have to address it. If you go too far with him and allow him to do too much and the team is not performing because you've overdone that, then you have to come down hard on that individual.

Freshmen weren't even allowed to play until 1972, so starting a freshman running back in 1980 was still a new concept. In fact, Herschel was officially fourth string going into the opening game at Tennessee. How did you process through the decision to let him play, and did you feel it was important for him to earn his right to start in front of everyone?

I felt like he had to earn his right. We had good seniors – good leadership there. We had a good solid team, and Herschel was the missing piece of the puzzle to complete the team. He came in with such high praise, and I tempered that. I wasn't going to give him anything. He had to earn everything.

He earned that early on in practice by the way he conducted himself. He was not a prima donna. He was a hard worker, and he was such a good example that the players gradually respected him, even though early on, they were going to put the test to him. They were reading in the newspapers about this superstar as well.

I did not start him in the first game against Tennessee because I had two tailbacks that had been around a good while. I had a plan where each one would have two series. I was going to give Herschel an opportunity to see if he could blend in. I knew he was going to be a great player, but the question was, "How soon?"

The other two tailbacks did pretty well, but when Herschel came in, he absolutely earned that position in front of his teammates, coaches, and fans. Because of that, he started the second half. I felt it was important that he earn that right in front of everyone.

With Herschel being such a good example of a leader, did you point young players to him when they came to Georgia?

You don't really have to say that. It was pretty obvious because of the way he conducted himself in a positive way, and he performed. The rest of the players saw that. Some of the best leaders are those that are great examples. They don't have to say a lot, but the way they conduct themselves speaks volumes, as with Herschel.

After you won the national championship in Herschel's first season, the media scrutiny on your program and on your superstar increased greatly going into the next season. How did you tune all that out and keep your team and your running back focused on the field?

It was challenging. We lost one of our top coaches, Erk Russell, who went down to Georgia Southern and was a great coach. The team responded and won two other SEC championships. However, we didn't win the national championship again. But we had the best record in the country (43-4) in those four years, including one year without Herschel. That shows you the kind of team we had in addition to Herschel. He came along at a great time, but he'll be the first to tell you that he had a great supporting cast.

It's common now, but back in the early 1980s it was relatively rare for a player to leave early for professional football. How did you handle Herschel leaving before his senior year for the USFL? Do you think he made the right decision?

I think that Herschel enjoyed the attention and flirted with the opportunities he had. He was even talking about going to the Canadian League as a freshman. Every year there was a challenge. There were all kinds of secret goings-on that we weren't aware of in those days – primarily, agents getting to players without our knowledge. Because of his performance, he was approached and tempted more than any player in the country during those times.

When he went to the USFL, he got himself in a trap that he couldn't get out of – though he tried, and they closed the door on him. I think deep down, if he looks back on it, he would like to have finished his fourth year. He even had a press conference saying that he was coming back until it came out that he had signed a contract with the USFL.

They'd promised him that if he didn't want to do it by the next morning, they'd tear up the contract that he'd signed with those stipulations. Well, they tore it up, but they also made a copy of it and then leaked it to the media. So he was led into a trap. Had he completed his fourth year, he would have set a rushing record that would have never been broken. He's still in the top 20 all-time rushing leaders, and he only played three years.

So even though Herschel left under all of that controversy, the 1983 season was still highly successful, with your only loss being to No. 3 Auburn by six points. How did the team rally together after losing a big player like that?

They were a solid bunch of athletes, and they bonded as a team even without Herschel. Had he been there, I'm sure we would have beaten Auburn and won our fourth straight SEC championship. We had a good group of athletes who were highly motivated and who wanted to prove that they could win without him. The downside of having Herschel was that we couldn't sign a great tailback during the time he was here, so we were without a top tailback the year after he left. Yet we finished fourth in the nation and had a great team.

It's common these days for athletes to leave school early for the NFL. Do you think players should always stay through their senior year? How would you handle those conversations if you were coaching today?

I think each one is different. Some are much more mature than the average player, many of whom are susceptible to worrying about injuries (which is a legitimate worry) and would look at the dollar signs. Some have the foresight: The Mannings are an example; they have a daddy that said it would be worth the risk to be there for four years in order to benefit from the complete college experience. Georgia also had two running backs recently who were mature in that respect, Nick Chubb and Sony Michel, who decided to come back for their fourth years.

It depends on the individual, his situation at home, how mature he is, and how beneficial it would be to make that decision. It's his decision, and you have to let him make it. You can only counsel with him to try to show him the benefits of coming back and also the risk of coming back in terms of injuries. It's most important that the player knows that you genuinely have his best interest at heart and not your own.

Vince Dooley Career Stats

Career Record – 201-77-10

National Championships – 1

Conference Titles – 6

Consensus All-Americans – 12

Heisman Trophy Winners – 1 (Herschel Walker 1982)

Bobby Dodd Coach of the Year – 1976

AFCA, Eddie Robinson, Sporting News, Walter Camp, FWAA Coach of the Year – 1980

College Football Hall of Fame – 1994

Amos Alonzo Stagg Award – 2001

"Bear" Bryant Lifetime Achievement Award – 2010

Intangibles

CHAPTER 9

Frank Girardi

LOYALTY

"Players need to know that you think more of them than just winning football games. When players know that when they come to your school they're going to be treated fairly, it becomes a place they want to go."

For 36 years, Frank Girardi put this quote in his offensive and defensive playbooks:

> *If you work for a man, in heaven's name work for him, speak well of him, and stand by the institution he represents. Remember, an ounce of loyalty is worth a pound of cleverness. If you must growl, condemn, and eternally find fault — resign your position, and when you are outside, damn to your heart's content — but as long as you are part of the institution, do not condemn it. If you do, the first high wind that comes along will blow you away, and probably you will never know why. — Elbert Hubbard*

Loyalty. It's a word that perfectly applies to Frank Girardi. He spent 36 years as the Lycoming College Head Coach. A Division III school in Williamsport, Pennsylvania, Lycoming had 29 straight winning seasons under Girardi. He's one of only 17 coaches at any level to have won more than 250 games at the same school.

Photo courtesy of Lycoming Athletics.

Girardi's loyalty to Lycoming resulted in 12 MAC Coach of the Year awards and 13 conference titles. He took over the job as a 33-year-old in 1972 and retired in 2007. He's been inducted into four halls of fame.

Girardi played running back for West Chester University in Pennsylvania. He was inducted into the College Football Hall of Fame as a coach in 2016 and is the first CFB Hall inductee from Lycoming.

What made you want to go into coaching?

Back when I was deciding where to go to college, I was influenced strongly by my high school coaches. I played sports all my life up through high school and then looked at what I wanted to do. I knew I wanted to be involved somehow through sports. My coach told me about some schools that were interested in me that had good physical-education programs, and he agreed that coaching would be a good vocation for me. I know that sounds different from nowadays, but I certainly took it to heart when he said those things. I certainly don't regret it because of all of the positives that we get from coaching.

When you first start coaching, you're doing it because you think you can make a contribution. But when you really get into coaching, you know that the contribution you make is really trying to develop these guys – help them develop values that are going to define them – and you try to have a positive impact. That doesn't come immediately, but once you're in it, you realize that's the reason for it. The wins are great – don't get me wrong. But it's the other things that are the most rewarding.

Coaches Who Influenced Me

High school: Tom Vargo

College: Glenn Killinger

Coaching Clinics: Vince Lombardi

What lessons did you learn from these guys?

Any time that you work with or for people, you don't agree with everything they do. But you agree with a lot of things, and you try to take the things that you think will be successful for you and your personality and you use them. I went to many clinics to learn from other coaches, and a lot of those coaches had influence on me. I remember when Vince Lombardi said at a clinic that coaching was the same no matter where you coach. He said he always taught technique, no matter if he was coaching junior high or professional. I remember that like it was yesterday.

What was your favorite part about being a coach?

I've said this on many occasions: It was the locker room. If you've played the game, you know what I'm talking about. The day-to-day interaction with those guys. That was something that I certainly missed, and I'm still close with my guys. Obviously winning and losing were very important, but that day-to-day interaction, that was the most important thing.

To be perfectly honest with you, though, that wasn't the most important thing to me when I started. I was too focused on surviving and winning games, and I was fortunate enough to win. But as time went by, I realized what was more important.

What was the hardest part?

The hardest part is that everybody can't play. I had great kids on my team, outstanding young men, but sometimes they aren't able to make it. Some of the kids that I'm closest to (I call them "kids" – they're in their 50s now) weren't regular players. I used to have a saying that hard work doesn't guarantee success. There are many other things that go along with it. Without hard work, it's not going to happen, but it doesn't guarantee it. It was tough seeing kids that wanted to play, but just weren't able to do it.

What is the No. 1 piece of advice that you would give a young coach?

I would say that you have to develop trust and be yourself. Make sure the game isn't about you; it's about the players. Treat all of them as you would have liked to be treated at that age. I used to tell my assistants all the time to remember how they were when they were 18 or 19 years old. Make sure you talk to kids as individuals, and don't be so quick to make negative decisions about kids.

Why does football matter?

I think it's the greatest team sport there is. You can develop a lot of other qualities and a lot of traits in other sports, but the traits that you're going to develop and the values that you're going to get in football are going to define you as a person. Football, to me, has no comparison. The things that you're learning are going to be part of your life. You're going to be judged by others on the values that define you, whether it's loyalty, responsibility, pride – you name it. It's a great sport. You get so much out of it that's going to help you throughout your life.

The greatest thrill for me is when I get together with my guys and they tell me about things I said to them that they still remember. That's so gratifying, to know that they're thinking about things that I said that made some sense to them.

LOYALTY

What made you want to stay in the same place for so long? Did you have offers to go elsewhere throughout your career?

When I got the head job here, I was 33. It was a great thing because I grew up in Willamsport, Pennsylvania, and that's where Lycoming College is. So when I got that job, I was like the hometown guy coming back home. That was really gratifying. The townspeople and fans were just outstanding. It was a great place for the kids to grow up.

Later on, I became the Athletics Director as well as the Head Coach. I had friends and family here, so when other opportunities came up, I didn't think it was a good idea to leave when my kids were in school. As my kids got older and I got other opportunities, I turned those down because, when it really came down to it, I had it good here – I liked where we lived, I liked our lifestyle, I liked our friends – and so I turned them down, even though they were bigger schools.

What were the benefits of staying in the same place? Did it help in recruiting?

Absolutely. I remember one time there were rumors that I was going to coach a Division I-AA school. I immediately had to call all my recruits and tell them it wasn't true. Believe it or not, when you get to these parents, they want to know how long you're going to stay. Liking the place where I was so much helped us in our recruiting. My staff was made up of many guys that played for me. The fact that we had continuity on our staff meant that we were together on virtually everything. Parents liked the fact that we were going to be here. Even when I got older, we found out that kids wanted to come to a place with stability.

How did you make sure that you weren't getting complacent? Did you make big changes, or were you consistent with your philosophy throughout your tenure?

I think we were fairly consistent with our style, but you have to be flexible – certainly, with the way the game changed. Back in the '70s and '80s, there wasn't a spread offense or zone reads. When those things came in the game, we decided we had to recruit kids that could do those types of things.

Our basic principles stayed the same though. Being able to communicate with players was important, and I think that's lacking now. If you can't communicate with players and you can't get players to trust you, then you're going to have a tough time. If you can do that, they'll go to the wall for you.

So, we didn't change in that aspect, but we did change philosophically on offense and defense. I think you do have to change with the times. That's what we tried to do, and we recruited kids to fit into that scheme.

What advice would you give to a coach that's trying to build trust amongst players?

You have to prove it to the players. I always had an open-door policy, which meant that a kid could come in and talk to me about anything. If he wanted it to be confidential, it was confidential. There are so many ways that you can build trust. If you say that we're practicing only an hour one day, then you practice an hour and a half that day, that's not building trust.

Players need to know that you think more of them than just winning football games. You need to try to help them get jobs and things like that. Once you start that and do that, then the word is out to the high school coaches. When players know that when they come to your school they're going to be treated fairly, it becomes a place they want to go.

You have to be able to listen to kids, too. I used to have an informal meeting with the captains in my office once a week. I would ask if there was something that I should be aware of. When they bring up a suggestion about something, you have to listen.

I remember in spring ball one time, the captains came to me and had a unique request. They said that the upcoming Saturday was the start of fishing season, and we had about eight or 10 guys that wanted to go home to fish with their dads. Now this was April, and I had to think, "If I give one Saturday off in April, will that affect whether we win in November?"

So I told them they could have the day off, and you would have thought they'd won the lottery. It's the little things like that.

Frank Girardi Career Stats

Career Record – 257-97-4

Conference Titles – 13

Playoff Appearances – 11

Consensus All-Americans – 13

Consecutive Winning Seasons – 29

College Football Hall of Fame – 2016

CHAPTER 10

Marino Casem

BALANCING DUTIES AS ATHLETICS DIRECTOR AND COACH

"As an Athletics Director, you have to coach everybody: students, faculty, administration, alumni, fans. You have to teach everybody what your program and your school are about. You're not just the football coach; you're everyone's coach."

No matter what your profession, you don't earn the nickname "The Godfather" without having achieved a special amount of success.

Marino "The Godfather" Casem certainly earned his nickname through his impressive success at Alcorn State and Southern University. After one season at Alabama State, in which he finished 2-8, Casem would move on to Alcorn State, where he would stay for 22 years and win seven Southwestern Athletic Conference (SWAC) titles, four black college national titles, and seven National Black College Coach of the Year awards.

But Casem wasn't just a successful coach. He spent over 30 years as an Athletics Director at Alcorn State and Southern, splitting his coaching and administrative duties most of that time.

The balancing act required to be a winning Head Coach and a winning administrator is impressive. Casem oversaw major athletic facility upgrades at Alcorn State and Southern and was widely regarded as one of the nation's finest athletics administrators.

Photo courtesy of Alcorn State Athletics.

Casem's 1984 Alcorn State team finished the season 9-0 and became the first black college to be voted the top team in Division I-AA. In his tenure as Head Coach for the Braves, he sent over 60 players to the National Football League.

He continued his administrative career after retiring from coaching in 1988 at Southern. He would lead the Jaguars to win six SWAC Commissioner's Cups before retiring in 1999.

Casem has served on numerous NCAA committees, has won several lifetime achievement awards, and is a member of eight halls of fame. He played center and linebacker at Xavier University of Louisiana and was inducted into the College Football Hall of Fame as a coach in 2003.

What made you want to go into coaching?

My wife got me into coaching; she got me my first job. As I graduated from Xavier University of Louisiana in 1956, I went to Tuskegee because they were training corrective therapists. After I finished the course, they said it would be six weeks before I found out if I passed and was certified. My fiancé at the time – we'd been dating throughout college – got a job at Utica Junior College in Mississippi as an assistant to the president. The assistant football coach there quit, and she asked the president of the college if he would interview me. I went down for an interview and got the job as an assistant coach.

Coaches Who Influenced Me

High School: WP Porter, Elmer Henderson

College: Alfred C. "Zac" Priestley

What is your favorite part about coaching?

It's something that's all or nothing. You've got to be totally dedicated. Whatever you've got to do, you need to rise to that occasion. It's the dedication and the discipline and the state of mind. It's an everyday affair.

What's the hardest part?

The hardest part about being a coach is putting in the time. It's an all-inclusive thing. It takes up your every thought, even when you're doing something else. The preparation and the attitude you have is always there. You're responsible for young lives. You're responsible for their well-being. You have to prepare yourself to be available at a moment's notice. You can prepare, but there are always adjustments going on. A kid might get sick. A kid might have a lapse of judgment. You've got to foresee that – though you can't prepare for some things, they just happen.

What is your No. 1 piece of advice for a young coach?

You've got to be prepared, and you've got to be motivated. It's an everyday affair. You can't turn it on and turn it off. It's all about preparation. You've got to be able to adjust to whatever happens. Coaching prepares you for life. It prepares you to adjust at a moment's notice.

Never be outworked. I don't care if you have more talent – if you're bigger, stronger, and faster than me. You'll never outwork me, you'll never out-prepare me, you'll never be more meticulous. I can't overemphasize the idea that you can never be outworked.

Why does football matter?

There's a fine line between love and hate. That line is respect. It teaches a young man to love somebody. You have to play for somebody: your mother and your daddy, your sweetheart, your neighbor, your uncle, your favorite aunt. You learn respect. A coach has to show his players respect and trust. A coach has to be fair and friendly, but firm. You have to tell your players the truth, but also listen to them. And you have to care – I mean, really care.

BALANCING DUTIES AS ATHLETICS DIRECTOR AND HEAD COACH

Being a head football coach is a full-time job, and being an Athletics Director is a full-time job. How do you balance the two and make sure you spend enough time on each?

It's all about preparation. As Athletics Director, you have to tell your coaches that they're responsible for their players. They have to be disciplined. They can't be overbearing. The AD also needs to let the coaches know that you're there for them. Every penny and every resource that you have must be open to them. They need the materials with which they need to work.

What are some practical ways that you can help the coaches of every sport as the Athletics Director?

You have to have an open-door policy with your coaches. They need to know they can come to you at any time. You can never be underprepared. You've got to know that the name of the game is recruiting, retention, and graduation. As an Athletics Director, you have to coach everybody: students, faculty, administration, alumni, fans. You have to teach everybody what your program and your school are about. You're not just the football coach; you're everyone's coach. You need to use your power of influence, but you also need to listen to everyone.

And you need to make clear to the coaches that they're not just there to coach their particular sport; they're there to teach the kids to be scholar-athletes, and they're also responsible for every student and piece of equipment in their charge. They can't just coach the kids from four to six in the evening; they have to be aware of what the kid's doing in the classroom. They have to be responsible for them. That's the Head Coach for every sport. You're responsible for the well-being of the students in your charge. See if they go to class, if they get enough to eat, if they get medical care. See if they studied today, and see what their home environment is. Coaching is all-involved, no matter what the sport.

As Athletics Director, you've got to be tuned in well to what the other coaches – baseball, basketball, tennis, etc. – are doing. You have to see that the coaches are getting the help, equipment, and support they need to operate. Being at a small college, we often adhered to the saying, "We've done so much with so little for so long, we think we can do anything with nothing."

When you transitioned away from coaching into full-time administration, what did you miss the most?

I missed the camaraderie and the interactions with students. I missed the good times. The highs are so high; the lows are so low. The valleys and hills. I missed that competition. You'd compete hard against the guy on the other side of the field. You'd be a warrior during the game, but then after the game was over, that guy across the 50-yard line becomes your best friend. So, I really missed that part of the game.

Marino Casem Career Stats

Career Stats – 159-93-8

National Championships – 4

Conference Titles – 7

Outstanding Contributor to Amateur Football Award – 1998

College Football Hall of Fame – 2003

National Association of Collegiate Directors of Athletics Hall of Fame – 2006

CHAPTER 11

Mike Bellotti

LIFE AND WORK AFTER COACHING

"For me, being able to stay close to the game and watch the game – but without the pressure of winning and losing – is great. It allows me to enjoy the game. I can share a little bit of what I know with the viewers."

Oregon Ducks football is known for flashy jerseys, high-powered offenses, and a consistent, winning culture. For the jerseys, you can thank Nike founder and Oregon alum Phil Knight. For the high-powered offense and the winning culture, look no further than Mike Bellotti.

Bellotti, who coached the Ducks for 14 seasons, led Oregon to its first four ten-win seasons in history. Though the team's biggest success, making it to the BCS national championship game in 2010, would come two years after his retirement and under his successor Chip Kelly, it was Bellotti who established Oregon as a college football destination.

His first five head-coaching years were spent at Chico State before becoming the Oregon offensive coordinator under Head Coach Rich Brooks in 1989.

When Bellotti retired as Oregon Head Coach in 2008, he ascended to the role of Oregon Athletics Director, but after nine months on the job, he resigned to go to work for ESPN as a college-football analyst, a role he still holds today.

Photo courtesy of Eric Evans/GoDucks.com.

It is in this role that Bellotti has thrived in his post-coaching career, covering the national college-football scene as a color commentator for games and working as a studio analyst.

Bellotti, who played tight end for the University of California-Davis, was inducted into the College Football Hall of Fame as a coach in 2014.

What made you want to go into coaching?

I enjoyed playing multiple sports in high school. At the college level, I had to select between football, basketball, and baseball. I chose football because it came first and trumped everything else, and I was a better football player than a basketball player. I played collegiate football and a tremendous amount of intramural sports. I truly believe in the benefits of being a multi-sport athlete, and now there's a lot of proven research that you're a better all-around athlete if you play multiple sports.

I was actually a pre-med major for three years, but really, I didn't want to do that. My parents wanted me to be a doctor, and it was the same curriculum as physical education. Finally, my senior year I wanted to take an upper-division PE class, and they said I couldn't do it since I wasn't a PE major, so I changed my major as a senior to PE. My intent was to teach and coach in high school. I think the longer you're involved in a sport, the more you come to appreciate what the sport has done for you from a growth standpoint and a perspective standpoint. You learn how to cooperate, compete, lead, and push yourself and your teammates in football, and you learn what team is all about.

Many coaches recognize that coaching is the only way to continue their involvement in football once their careers end. That was exactly what I did my first year out of college. I got my teaching credentials, and I coached at UC-Davis, where I'd played for four years. I was coaching people I'd just played with, which was interesting. During that time, I got a full-time high school teaching job as a track-and-field and basketball coach.

After one year of teaching high school, I knew that wasn't what I thought it would be. I wanted to coach college football. I went from earning $10,000 a year down to earning $1,000 a year. My dad asked me if I was crazy, and I said, "Yeah, probably."

I coached as a very underpaid coach at UC-Davis for four years. I was a football coach, and the last year I also coached baseball. It convinced me that it was what I wanted to do.

I went into coaching because I loved the game. I loved the people. I loved what the game stood for. I loved the competitive nature of the game, the mental aspect, the chess match of game day and calling plays. Until I became the Head Coach at Oregon, I called the plays everywhere I coached, but I recognized that as a Head Coach, you have other responsibilities. The most difficult decision of my coaching life was giving up play calling.

Coaches Who Influenced Me

High School: Dick Ryan, Kent Robie

College: John Pappa (freshman coach), Jim Sochor (CFB Hall 1999), Tim Tierney, Pete Riehlman

Colleagues: Rich Brooks, Charlie Waters, Nick Aliotti, Jeff Tedford, Chip Kelly, Dirk Koetter, Denny Schuler, Neal Zoumboukos, Chris Petersen, Don Sawyer

What are some things you learned from these men?

I learned how to handle people and situations. I learned how to organize recruiting and how to recruit. It's very important to be active with the recruiting situations, to educate your coaches on what to look for from a physical, mental, and emotional standpoint. How are they off the field? Do they have a good football IQ? Are they good people? Do they do the things on the field that we feel they'll need to do to be successful at this level?

What was your favorite part about coaching?

It was three things: Being involved with young people and seeing them grow – the boys-to-men concept. Seeing them mature and become confident, stronger, wiser, and more proficient.

Two, the camaraderie of the coaching staff. I don't think there's anything that beats being in the locker room after a hard-fought win and singing the fight song with your team, your coaches, and your staff. There's almost nothing in the world that can compare to that feeling.

Finally, the challenge of competition. When you're out there physically putting your limbs on the line every time and protecting your teammates and then finding a way to come away victorious, that's an amazing feeling. Not much can compare to that. That's why I always tell people to go play at a school where they can actually play and be a part of the team.

What was the hardest part of coaching?

When you have to tell somebody they aren't good enough. Or when you have to call a parent to tell them that their son is hurt and might have to have surgery. Or when you have to tell them they can't play again. Or when a young man gets in trouble and you have to call their parents to tell them that their son's going to be suspended or kicked off the team.

I believe we're educators first and foremost. We're looking beyond four years in college. We're looking to make better people. We're teaching young men how to be great teammates. We want them to know how to compete, to understand winning and losing, and to be able to handle both with class and dignity.

What is the No. 1 piece of advice that you would give to a young coach?

It took me ten years to learn this: Listen to your players. We all think we can win the battle just with X's and O's. But as the saying goes, it's getting those X's and O's to the "Johnnies and the Joes." It's those young men and what they know, what they can execute and what they can accomplish. It's all about what they like and how they think and what they can understand. Coaches will be more successful early on if they listen to their players and accept feedback.

Why does football matter?

I think football matters because it's one of the true tests of manhood. The reality of the challenge is to physically be tough and not let fatigue slow you down. There's a personal toughness and resilience that will help you the rest of your life. Many times you'll need to push forward, even if you're not 100 percent.

You learn to understand what it's like to compete for the highest prize, to be better the next play than you were the first play. You have to find a way to win or to be successful no matter what.

You also benefit by learning to understand cooperation and competition. For example, the offensive line operates as a cooperative unit. We all need to work together, and when we do, things go well.

Communication is so important in everything you do. Under duress, in the heat of the game, to be able to say something that's immediately understandable and relevant is so important to your staff, your team, and your teammates.

LIFE AND WORK AFTER COACHING

When your coaching/administration career came to an end, did you know what you wanted to do?

I don't know that we ever think that we're going to stop coaching. Fortunately, I was able to make that decision for myself. I said that I wanted to spend some more time with my family, and I needed to get my knees replaced. So it was a fairly easy decision for me at the time.

It's tough because the job now is more than 24/7/365. With recruiting and supervisorial responsibilities for staff and team, it's really an imposition on your family. You have to be ready for it, and you must have a wife and children that understand that they're not going to see you very much sometimes.

I went from football coach to Athletics Director, which used to be the natural progression of a football coach. It's a totally different world now, but what I found out was that as AD, I was fine during football season, but during the off-season, I wasn't. I just didn't love the other sports (other than basketball) like I loved football. I missed football. I missed the ability to talk and think about football.

I had the great fortune to work with our regional TV station and did color commentary for our games. I was doing the football broadcast during the game, but before and after the game and at halftime, I'd do my Athletics Director duties and spend time with the boosters in the suite.

I was able to get a little taste of TV work doing that, and I liked it. For me, being able to stay close to the game and watch the game – but without the pressure of winning and losing – is great. It allows me to enjoy the game. I can share a little bit of what I know with the viewers.

I was able to take advantage of my knowledge, transitioning from coaching football to talking about football; I still consider this as part of my football life. So I'm going on 48 years in the game of college football. I learn every day because the game changes. It helps me to stay young.

Is it for everybody? No. Some coaches really still want to coach, and they use broadcasting to get back to coaching and that's fine. In broadcasting, there's no winning or losing. It's a much steadier feeling than experiencing the highs and lows of actual coaching.

Being around the game so much, does it make you miss coaching even more?

Honestly, I miss it every day. I get asked that question often, and I always say that I miss it every single day, but not enough to go back. I really miss Friday night because that was message night, the calm before the storm. I miss Saturday because that was the game and actual competition. And I miss Sunday morning because we were pretty successful, and I usually enjoyed those days.

I don't miss recruiting. I loved being able to present our program and go into people's homes and talk about Oregon, but I don't miss the travel. We became a national recruiting organization, so I was on the road a ton. And there's always a lot of disappointment in college recruiting because you remember the ones that got away. Now I can talk about recruiting on Signing Day and not have to worry about whether I'll lose a guy to another program. Plus, the graduate transfer rules have changed college football.

How did you know it was time to walk away and if you had made the correct decision?

I don't know if you ever know if it's the right decision at the time. My mantra has always been that it takes two years to know if the decision was right. You can't judge that in the here and now. The first year you're unsure, and everything's new. By the second year, you know how you feel and if the decision was right. For me, I wasn't pressured to leave. I just recognized that it's a young man's game. Even though I still had the energy, I just wasn't as focused as I wanted to be.

The year after I left, we had a great team and went to the Rose Bowl, and then the next year I was working for

ESPN when Oregon went to the national championship game. Even though it was primarily my players and coaches, I didn't feel like I'd made a mistake, stepped away too soon, or that it should have been me coaching that team. I was proud of them, but I wasn't envious.

I got offered coaching jobs every single year, significant jobs in almost every major conference (SEC, B1G, PAC12, B12), but I turned them down. I wanted to spend time with my kids and grandkids.

I think everybody knows and has a feeling of what the right time is. Now if I go back and coach, I'll go back to a high school or a D-III team. I don't need 100,000 people in the stands. I'm going to coach for my relationship with coaches and players and my love of and respect for the game. I'm fortunate that I can put myself in that situation.

I've been working for ESPN for eight years now, and it's great because it allows me to stay involved, but doesn't require the year-round time commitment. I work for about six months, and the other six months are taken up with golf, tennis, pickle ball, a little fly-fishing, and family travel.

What are some lessons you've learned about how to be a good analyst that you would tell someone who is just starting out?

I think there are three things to focus on: You have to have a delivery that commands attention. Whether it's your voice or the way you say it, you have to be decisive and dynamic. You also have to be able to simplify what's happening on the field so you can appeal to the average fan. You don't have to dumb things down. It's just that in a football team meeting, we may have 30 minutes to explain something to our team. But on TV, you might have 10–15 seconds. So you have to be succinct.

You have to be a great communicator. You have to say a lot with a few words that paint a picture for your audience. Analysts are anticipating what's going to happen next. There are so many things the viewer doesn't see or understand about a play that just happened, but the networks want more foresight and foreshadowing of what's going to happen next.

Another practical thing is you need to practice talking with a voice in your head. The people in your earpiece will be telling you one thing while you're talking about another thing. You have a voice inside your head controlling the time frame and letting you know how long you have to speak, or where they want to go with your next comment.

But it's pretty similar to being on the headphones as a coach when you're calling plays and other coaches are talking in your ear. I guess coaches have been multitasking for years.

Mike Bellotti Career Stats

Career Record – 137-80-2

Conference Titles – 2

Consensus All-Americans – 1

College Football Hall of Fame – 2014

CHAPTER 12

Steve Spurrier

STANDING OUT

"There are two ways to be successful in life: One is to do it like everybody else and to outwork them. The other is to do it differently. I chose to be different."

Steve Spurrier is, in a word, different. He dressed differently, talked differently, and, most importantly, coached differently than any other coach before or after him.

And, he insists, it was mostly by design. He didn't become the "Head Ball Coach" by accident.

The visor, the golf shirt, the sayings, the points.

All of those were purposeful choices Spurrier made to stand out. Not only did they help him get noticed, they helped him become an icon, and they put his programs on the map. From success at Duke, to dominance at Florida, to consistent winning at South Carolina, Spurrier's ability to stand out helped him change the course of three different football programs.

But behind all that character is perhaps the greatest combination of player and coach in college football history. The 1966 Heisman Trophy winner played quarterback for ten years in the NFL before joining the coaching ranks, where he coached Duke University, the Tampa Bay Bandits of the USFL, the University of Florida, the NFL's Washington Redskins, and the University of South Carolina.

Photo courtesy of UAACommunications.

His "Fun 'n' Gun" offense, led by 1996 Heisman Trophy winner and College Football Hall of Famer Danny Wuerffel, took the Gators to their first national championship in 1996. That team led the nation in scoring and helped usher in a new, high-scoring, era of college football.

Spurrier won eight conference titles during his career – seven at Florida and one at Duke. Wuerffel made him the first Heisman Trophy winner to coach a Heisman Trophy winner himself. He's the winningest coach in both Florida and South Carolina history.

Spurrier was inducted into the College Football Hall of Fame as a player in 1986. In 2017, Spurrier became the fourth person to join the HOF as both a player and a coach, joining Amos Alonzo Stagg, Bobby Dodd, and

Bowden Wyatt. Spurrier is the only one of the four to have played after World War II.

What made you want to go into coaching?

My path was quite different from almost everyone else's. I was fortunate enough to be in the NFL for 10 years. I was the backup for eight years, so I didn't get beaten up too much. But obviously you can't play football forever. After my pro days, I had to get a job. Back in those days, we didn't make quite as much money as they do these days, so we couldn't retire at the age of 30.

I really had no plans for what I was going to do, but while I was watching the Gators play football after my playing career was over, it hit me that if I could be a coach, it would be fun, it would not seem like working, and I could be on a team. Being a part of a team is something that we all need to do.

Fortunately, Coach Doug Dickey hired me at Florida to be a QB coach. Unfortunately, we didn't win enough games, and he was fired at the end of the season, and I was out of a job for a full month. I didn't know people in the coaching business that could possibly hire me.

And then Pepper Rodgers at Georgia Tech, who had coached me my sophomore year in college, had a QB coach leave for another job, so he called me. I interviewed for the job and got hired, but then we didn't win enough games there either! So after two years, he was fired, and I was out of a job again.

But I had met the Duke University coach that summer, and I got a chance to be the offensive coordinator. I was in my third year of coaching when I got that job, but it probably was my last chance. Fortunately, we had back-to-back winning seasons, and I got offered the chance to be a Head Coach at age 37 in the USFL. Somehow, I lasted 30 years in the profession.

Most of everything I learned about coaching I learned after I became a coach. I didn't learn much at all about coaching when I was a player. I was blessed along the way. If you can win at Duke University, then you have a chance to be successful anywhere.

When I got hired as the Head Coach at Duke in 1987, one person told the Athletics Director that if they hired me as the Head Coach, I would win a bunch of games and leave. And the AD said, "If I hire Steve Spurrier and he wins a bunch of games and leaves, then he'll be the first coach in Duke history to do that."

Fortunately, we had that big year in 1989 when we won the ACC championship, and the Florida head-coaching job opened up. I got the chance to coach at my alma mater.

Coaches Who Influenced Me

High School: Kermit Tipton (football), Elvin Little (basketball), John Broyles (baseball)

College: Ray Graves

Colleagues: Doug Dickey (CFB Hall 2003), Pepper Rodgers, Red Wilson, Mike McGee

What were the characteristics of these coaches that you appreciated and learned from?

My high school football coach wasn't loud, but he was direct and a really good motivator. Our team was ready to play all the time. We were up for every game, but for some reason, we lost a bunch of close games. We were one of the best teams in the state and were co-conference champions one year (there wasn't a state playoff in those days). We had winning teams all the time.

In basketball, we would win our conference every year, but we didn't get to the state tournament. Our coach was a fiery guy who yelled a little bit, but mostly he was encouraging. I coached more like him than any of my other coaches. He hated losing and was demonstrative.

In baseball, we just couldn't lose. We won back-to-back state championships my junior and senior year. Our coach was the history teacher at the high school, a very quiet individual. I never saw him mad, and I don't think I ever heard him raise his voice. We just had a bunch of kids that had played with and against each other since Little League. We found a way to win just about every game, and when playoffs came around, we won every game.

My college coach, Ray Graves, was a wonderful man that really showed concern for all his players.

Those guys influenced the way I was as a coach. But specifically learning how to coach was down to studying books from legends like John Wooden, Vince Lombardi, and Bear Bryant.

What was your favorite part about being a coach?

The thing about coaching is that you're on a team and you get to celebrate with a lot of people. I've always said football is the greatest of team sports because it takes everyone doing their job for the team to be successful. When your star players are some of the best teammates, then you really have a chance to have championship seasons. That was certainly what we had here at Florida with our quarterbacks Shane Matthews and Danny Wuerffel. We won six SEC championships in a seven-year period. Our star players were certainly good guys, and we had outstanding teamwork all of those years.

What was the hardest part?

When everybody can't play and some players are a little bit upset. There wasn't ever a real, real hard part. Recruiting is what it is. I never thought I was the greatest recruiter in the world, even though we had some really good recruiting classes here at Florida and some good ones in South Carolina. You've got to have good players to win. You can have good players and not win, but to be successful you've got to start with assembling the players. There's a reason Alabama is the best team in the country – they have the best recruiting class every year.

What is your No. 1 piece of advice for a young coach?

First of all, don't use profanity. I don't know why coaches think they have to use profanity. That was something that I didn't allow on the practice field or in games or anywhere. You don't have to curse or yell at the officials or things like that. Show some class.

Second, make sure your team is in the best condition that they can possibly be in. John Wooden would say that conditioning will kick in before the first half is over. In football, it kicks in during the second quarter.

Those two things are what we all can do no matter the players we have.

Third thing is to try to build your own identity. Don't be afraid to be a little bit different from everybody else. One reason I survived at Duke University was because I tried to coach differently than everybody else in the ACC. We had to have our own special way of running our offense, and it had to be good and it had to be exact. We used to open the game with the no-huddle offense, and the reason I liked doing that was because nobody else was doing it.

Someone asked me why I wore a visor, and I said, "Because nobody else was."

I tried not to talk the way every other coach talked. I wasn't a coach that bragged about how hard I worked. Everybody works hard. I would try to emphasize the success our teams had had and how good our players were. I believed in building our players up – not too high – but to let our players know that we had a chance to really have a successful season. I didn't want to poor-mouth the team too much. That was in style in the early '90s. Coaches didn't want to put pressure on their team to win the championship, but I wanted to say that our team had a chance if we played well.

Why does football matter?

It teaches you teamwork and the ability to get along and be responsible and accountable to everyone. It teaches you to show respect to your coaches and opponent and how to be an excellent teammate. Those players that are really good teammates and love all their coaches and teammates, those are the guys that become successful in life.

We can't play a sport our entire lives. Careers as athletes are very short, especially when you realize that most all of us are going to live until at least 80. Our athletic careers are very short compared to that, but the lessons we learn are lessons that can take us through any company or organization that we're involved with through the rest of our lives.

STANDING OUT

How did you stand out in your career?

There are two ways to be successful in life: One is to do it like everybody else and to outwork them. The other is to do it differently. I chose to be different.

So I just looked and listened. I decided I wanted to look and sound different. When I was at Florida, most of the SEC coaches were wearing sports coats and ties in those days. I put on the golf shirt, and now most coaches wear that today.

And I tried to talk a little differently. Most coaches use the words "great" and "football" all the time, so I started trying to find some new adjectives: outstanding, excellent, super, amazing, awesome, incredible, unbelievable, etc. I tried not to use that word "great" all the time, and I tried not to use "football" because everybody knows it's football. So I just used "ball."

"We got a good ball game going," I'd say, and things like that.

I didn't try to brag about how many hours we worked. People sort of thought we didn't work real hard. Well, we worked hard enough to win a bunch of championships, but we just didn't talk about it.

Did the desire to be different extend to your on-field choices?

Yeah, I think so. The year before I got to Florida, they had Emmitt Smith, who became the best running back in NFL history, and they had the third-best defense in the country. Yet they went 7-5.

I inherited that team. The receivers were already here, and the QB Shane Matthews was here but he hadn't taken a snap in two years. The third year that he was here, he was the SEC Player of the Year. All he needed was an opportunity and a little bit of coaching, so I inherited an extremely talented team.

On the opening drive of the first game of the season, we went no-huddle and Shane Matthews hit three big passes of about 20–25 yards each. Then we ran it in from about three or four yards. We scored within the first two minutes of the game, and the fans thought they might see that every possession. We didn't score 50 every game like we did that week. However, in 1996, Danny Wuerffel and his teammates did score at least 50 points in every home game. So we got there eventually.

The no-huddle offense, the ball in the air, and scoring – fans love to see scoring. Teams like to score; players like to score. The object is to win the game, but scoring is something everyone loves to do for some reason.

How much did being different help to build the brand of Florida?

Certainly the winning is the most important, but to score a lot of points and win is a little better. The reason I think it's better is because the backup players get to play. When we were here at Florida, we scored a lot of points. We generally led the conference in scoring, and we led the nation in 1996 when we won the national championship. When you get way ahead, all the backup players get to play, and all their parents are in the stands and everybody's happy. You come to practice the next week, and all the walk-on players and the backup players are happy because they got to play. If we had a bit of a down-the-line team coming up the next week, then the walk-ons and backup kids are pumped up because they know that they'll get to play if we get up by a lot.

Now, I know everyone can't get in that position. When I was at South Carolina, it was a little different because we didn't get way ahead like we did at Florida. But you need to make sure when you're ahead by a lot to get the backup players in because they don't practice all week to not play. We tried to really show some concern and welfare for the backup players also.

Was coaching at your alma mater different from coaching elsewhere?

I didn't really pay a whole lot of attention to that. In the same way, people would ask me how I felt about coaching South Carolina down in the Swamp against the Gators. I would say, "Hey, this is my team now."

I was the play caller all my years in college, so my mind is just concentrated on calling the best plays for my team. So even though I was coaching at my alma mater, it was all about the players. Because you become so close to the players through all the practices and workouts, you just want to do your job so they can do their job. I generally tried to think about what I could do to help our team play the best they could.

Steve Spurrier Career Stats

Career Record – 228-89-2

National Championships – 1

Conference Titles – 7

Consensus All-Americans – 16

Heisman Trophy Winners – 1 (Danny Wuerffel 1996)

College Football Hall of Fame – 1986 (as player), 2017 (as coach)

Acknowledgements

This book wouldn't have been possible without the enormous efforts of others – most importantly, my editor and writing mentor Jon Finkel, who guided me through the entire process. Jon was with me from the very beginning on this, kept me on track to finish, and helped me through all of the difficult and frustrating times.

Also helping me throughout were the good people at the National Football Foundation, especially Alan Cox who was always willing to help me with my requests.

Each and every coach was more than gracious with their time, but I want to specifically thank R.C. Slocum who was the first coach to respond to my interview request. Coach Slocum's willingness to participate helped legitimize the project, so I wanted to acknowledge him for taking a chance on me.

The SIDs, assistants, and photographers at each school were all vital to my efforts, specifically Claude Felton and Deanna Dooley at Georgia, Mike Houck and Julie Watson at OU, Brian Lucas and Linda Wilkins at Wisconsin, Joe Guistina at Lycoming, Robbie Kleinmutz at Alcorn State, Steve Rourke at UCLA, Andy McNamara at Oregon, Stephen Kwong Lee at Tennessee, Brad Marquardt and Alan Cannon at Texas A&M, Tim Casey and Jennifer Wagner at Florida, Keith Mann at Nebraska, and Troy Garnhardt at Air Force.

Working on this book has been a dream come true for a kid from East Texas who went to the University of Oklahoma to experience a big college football atmosphere. I never thought I would be privileged enough to be able to tell the stories of these legendary figures. I am eternally grateful to each of them, and I'm grateful to you, the reader. And lastly I'd like to thank my wife, Sami, for putting up with all of the late nights and being patient with me throughout.

ABOUT THE AUTHOR

Scott Bedgood has interviewed Hall of Famers, Emmy and Grammy award winners, Guinness World Record Holders, adventurers, and entrepreneurs in his journalism career. A sportswriter since he was 15-years-old working for the *Tyler Morning Telegraph* in Tyler, Texas, Bedgood attended the University of Oklahoma where his passion for college football compelled him to pursue a career covering the sport. Scott began covering college football after graduating and moving to Dallas where he lives with his wife Samantha. His other work can be found on his website scottbedgood.com.

CPSIA information can be obtained
at www.ICGtesting.com
Printed in the USA
LVOW07*2002141117

556261LV00011B/117/P